# The Coming of Rome

**Britain before the Conquest**
An Archaeological History of the British Isles,
c.1500 BC – AD 1066

General Editor: Andrew Wheatcroft

*The Origins of Britain*  Lloyd and Jennifer Laing
*Celtic Britain*  Lloyd Laing
*The Coming of Rome*  John Wacher
*Later Roman Britain*  Stephen Johnson
*Anglo-Saxon England*  Lloyd and Jennifer Laing

# The Coming of Rome

*John Wacher*

Routledge & Kegan Paul
London and Henley

*In memoriam H.S.W.*

Printed in U.S.A. by Arcata Graphics
Kingsport, TN.

*First published in 1979*
*by Routledge & Kegan Paul Ltd*
*39 Store Street, London WC1E 7DD and*
*Broadway House, Newtown Road,*
*Henley-on-Thames, Oxon RG9 1EN*
*Photoset in Palatino*
*and printed in Great Britain by*
*Lowe & Brydone Printers Ltd*
*Thetford, Norfolk*

*British Library Cataloguing in Publication Data*

*Wacher, John Stewart*

*The coming of Rome. – (Britain before*
*the conquest).*
*1. Great Britain – History – Roman*
*period, 55 B.C.–449 A.D.*
*I. Title      II. Series*
*936.1'04        DA145*

*ISBN 0 7100 0312 9*

# Contents

# Illustrations

## Photographs and drawings

(In captions to illustrations which show inscriptions, the following conventions have been used in transcriptions: ( ) enclose letters added to complete a word abbreviated in the text; [ ] enclose letters supposed to have been originally in the text but now totally illegible or lost.)

## Maps

## Figures

# Acknowledgments

The author and publishers are grateful to the following persons and institutions for permission to reproduce illustrations: Bath City Council, Roman Baths Museum, nos 44, 53, 67, 85, 100; Professor Dr J. E. Bogaers, no. 66; Canterbury Archaeological Trust, no. 87; Carlisle Museum and Art Gallery, no. 72; Cirencester Excavation Committee, nos 41, 82 (a), (b) and (d); The Clarendon Press, Oxford, and R. P. Wright, nos 50, 51; Colchester and Essex Museum, nos 12, 31, 68(d); The Committee for Aerial Photography, University of Cambridge, nos 5, 7, 8, 9, 15, 17 (a) and (b), 26, 32, 33, 34, 40, 42, 43; Norman Cook and the Wells Natural History and Archaeological Society, no. 69(b); Corinium Museum, Cirencester, nos 37, 69(c), 82(a) and (b), 84; Crown Copyright, reproduced by permission of the Comptroller of Her Majesty's Stationery Office, nos 22, 25, 39, 76, 77; G. B. Dannell and the Nene Valley Research Committee, no. 68(e); The Dean and Chapter, Durham Cathedral, no. 99; Phillip Dixon, nos 18, 19; The Fitzwilliam Museum, Cambridge, no. 70; Fototeca Unione, Rome, copyright E. Wasmuth, Tübingen, no. 30 (a) and (b); Gloucester Museum, no. 82(c); Grosvenor Museum, Chester, nos 55, 57, 63, 90(a), (b), (c) and (d), 94; Hereford City Museums, nos 91 (a), (b) and (c); The Hunterian Museum, University of Glasgow, no. 71; John Kent (photos Ray Gardiner), nos 1, 11, 13; Landesmuseum, Trier, no. 47; Leicestershire Museums, nos 81 (a) and (b); J. Lucas and the Rugby Archaeological Society, no. 69(e); Alan McWhirr, nos 82 (a) and (b); J. V. S. Megaw, nos 27, 28; The Museum of Antiquities, Newcastle University, nos 35, 56, 98; The Museum of London, nos 38 (a) and (b), 46, 73, 78, 79, 80 (a) and (b), 82 (e) and (f), 89, 96; The National Museum of Antiquities of Scotland, Edinburgh, nos 60, 92; The National Museum of Denmark, Copenhagen, no. 23; The National Museum of Wales, nos 24, 54, 62, 69(a) and 58 for which kind permission was granted by Lord Bledisloe; Norfolk Museums Service, Norwich Castle Museum, no. 75; Professor S. Panciera, Istituto di Epigrafia e Antichita Greche e Romane, Rome, no. 36; Brian Philp and the Kent Archaeological Rescue Unit, no. 52; Reading Museum and

Art Gallery, no. 83; Rijksmuseum van Oudheden, Leiden, nos 64, 65 (a), (b), (c) and (d); The Royal Commission on the Ancient and Historical Monuments of Scotland, no. 16; M. Seillier, Musée des Beaux-Arts et d'Archéologie, Boulogne, no. 61; F. H. Thompson, no. 4; The Trustees of the British Museum, nos 20, 21, 69(d), 74, 93, 95; Verulamium Museum, no. 6; The Vindolanda Trust, no. 88; Graham Webster, no. 86; J. J. Wilkes, no. 49; Peter Woods, no. 68(c); York Archaeological Trust, no. 63; The Yorkshire Museum, York, no. 97; Christopher Young and the Oxfordshire Museums Service, Woodstock, no. 68(a) and (b). The remaining, uncredited, photographs are taken from the author's collection.

The author is also grateful to the following for help in the preparation of the book: Cheryl McCormick for typing the manuscript, Pat O'Halloran for the line drawings, Marius Cooke for photographic services, and especially Richard Wright for very generously allowing the reproduction of the texts of many Romano-British inscriptions.

Map 1 Tribal Britain and north Gaul at the time of Julius Caesar

TAEZALI

CALEDONES

VACOMAGI

VENICONES

EPIDII

DAMNONII

VOTADINI

SELGOVAE

NOVANTAE

BRIGANTES

PARISI

DECEANGLI

CORNOVII

ORDOVICES

CORITANI

ICENI

DEMETAE

CATUVELLAUNI

TRINOVANTES

SILURES

DOBUNNI

ATREBATES

CANTII

DUROTRIGES

DUMNONII

BELGAE

BELLOVACI

0    50    100 miles

REDONES

OSISMI

PARISI

# Caesar and Britain

## Chapter one

Britain in the middle of the first century BC was still in its political infancy, by comparison with central Mediterranean countries, and even with Gaul. It is true that some semblance of a tribal system, of a type by then already well-established in Gaul, existed in the south-east, but it was as yet in a state of flux and largely undeveloped. Indeed, it had mainly come about by a succession of migrations of north Gaulish tribesmen to Britain, so that, at first, a degree of kinship, and even a limited political control, existed between communities on both sides of the Channel. It is not within the province of this book to examine the causes of these early migrations, but, by the time Julius Caesar was considering his British expeditions, it is possible to recognise, mainly by a study of the relevant coinage and other archaeological material, broad areas of tribal interest, such as the Catuvellauni of Hertfordshire, and their neighbours the Trinovantes of Essex and Suffolk.

During his campaigns in Gaul between 57 and 56 BC, Caesar was quick to learn of the affinities between Britons and Gauls, which yielded both military aid and a place of refuge for the latter in their resistance to Caesar's advances, as when the Armoricans of modern Brittany and Normandy, who had surrendered to Caesar in 57 BC, revolted in the following year. The close commercial contacts which they had with south-west Britain were then invoked to provide military assistance. After the revolt had been suppressed, this alliance caused Caesar to look across the Channel, possibly even reconnoitring the area from the sea, in which he could have made use of the extensive maritime knowledge of the Veneti, one of the tribes in the Armorican confederation.

If Caesar considered an invasion of Britain in 56, the idea had quickly to be put aside, for he was experiencing continued hostility in Gaul even as far north as the mouth of the Rhine, while invasion was being threatened by German tribes from across the river. In addition, one of his principal generals was still engaged in Aquitania. The German invasion was nevertheless contained and countered by a short Roman campaign over the Rhine. But it had taken time and

(a)  (b)  (c)

1 Coins: (a) *Gallo-Belgic C* (Mack no.30) and (b) *E* (Mack no.27). These gold staters were closely successive issues of the Ambiani of northern Gaul, covering the years between about 60 and 51 BC; it is possible that the whole coinage was called into being by Caesar's attack on the Belgae in 57 BC. The great bulk of this coinage was probably struck between 57 and 55 BC, much of it for export to south-east Britain in return for reinforcements of men and materials. During this period there was an appreciable fall in weight and fineness. Later coins, probably dating from 52 BC, are very poor things, and rarely found in Britain (see (e) below). They may be related to Belgic support for the revolt of Vercingetorix in that year.

(c) *British G* (Mack no.46). The flood of gold provided by the Belgic imports stimulated a little native coinage. Types are based on Gallo-Belgic C, but weights and fineness were significantly lower; the coinage is scanty and short-lived. This type may be Trinovantian, while other variants are attributable to the Iceni and Coritani.

(d) *British L* (Mack no.135). This important gold coinage comes from an inland centre north of the Thames. It is typologically ancestral to the issues of Tasciovanus from the mint of Verulamium, and has been called Catuvellaunian. The obverse design is reduced to a mere pattern but the horse of the reverse shows strongly naturalising tendencies. It probably dates from a time when Roman trade with Britain had introduced classical influences and perhaps

2

the autumn of 55 was approaching before Caesar was able to take practical steps personally to examine Britain.

It is clear from his own narrative that a reconnaissance in force was intended, as a prelude to a full-scale assault the following year, for the advancing season would allow no more. First came the need to acquire accurate information about the opposite coast, which, surprisingly, he was unable to obtain from native Gauls; so a single warship was despatched to survey the coast-line and to identify suitable landing places. Although the task was entrusted to a favourite tribune, it seems to have been carried out in haste and with less than normal efficiency, for it not only failed to locate the southern arm of the river Wantsum, but also, apparently, misreported on the harbour at Dover. Consequently, when later Caesar arrived off Dover early in the morning with a fleet of eighty transports, carrying two legions, he deemed it unsuitable for an opposed landing and ignored the river estuary, which later became one of the foremost harbours of Roman Britain. Instead, he sailed northwards up the Kentish coast and probably beached his ships in the neighbourhood of what is today the town of Walmer, which also marks the northward termination of the high chalk cliffs. The modern coast-line there is chiefly distinguished by its exposed, rapidly-shelving, shingle beaches, offering little protection to stranded shipping, and Caesar is sometimes criticised in retrospect for having chosen such an inhospitable place for his landing. But we must remember that much has changed since his day, and we cannot be certain of the physical conditions of the shore-line at the time of his landing. Sea-level was that much lower, relative to the land, than now, and it may be that the Goodwin Sands, some 6 km off-shore and known to have been there in Roman times, perhaps stood higher out of the sea, and so provided a more sheltered anchorage than do the Downs today in certain weather conditions. The beach itself was probably quite different, for nearby Sandwich Bay has seen the change from pure, level sand to shelves of shingle in the last forty years. But while no sensible modern commander, given Caesar's equipment, might care to land on Walmer beach today, conditions then are unlikely to have been so hostile, as the landing, after a slight

(d)     (e)     (f)

hesitation, was entirely successful. Unfortunately the cavalry, carried in a separate, smaller fleet, had been prevented by the weather from uniting with the main force. Consequently, Caesar was at once deprived of a decisive victory, as the fleeing Britons could not be pursued.

The cavalry were twice unfortunate. On their second attempt to reach Britain they were prevented from doing so by the combination of a violent storm and a spring tide, which, additionally, damaged many of the beached warships and transports of the main fleet. It is curious that Caesar was not informed of the phenomenon of spring and neap tides, having maintained a fleet in the Channel for some time, and his omission to take this factor into account nearly caused the complete failure of his first expedition to Britain. The anchorage in the Downs provides protection from winds from most quarters except those from north or south, so we may conclude that the gale came from one of these directions, thus forcing some of the cavalry transports to return to the continent.

Caesar was thus placed in a difficult position, which encouraged the native Britons to resume hostilities, even though they had already sued for peace. They surrounded and attacked a legion sent out to gather supplies of grain, but were beaten back by reinforcements arriving just in time. There followed a pitched battle outside the Roman camp, in which Caesar was victorious, although once more unable to pursue his enemy through lack of cavalry. But by then repairs had been effected to most of his damaged ships, and he decided at this juncture to withdraw from Britain before the onset of the equinoctial gales.

furnished a fresh supply of precious metal.

(e) *Commius* (Mack no.92). The coinage of this Commius derives from an extensive uninscribed issue of gold staters and quarter-staters found south of the Thames. These are broadly contemporary with British L (d) and are unlikely to be really early, in spite of the direct imitation of a continental model of the Gallic War period. The Commius who fled to Britain in 52 BC can be associated with a group of base gold staters and quarter-staters (Gallo-Belgic Xc1 and 2) of the Gallic War sequence; the inscribed coins could be twenty-five years later, and may or may not belong to the same man.

(f) *Cunobelinus* (Mack no.206). The 'King of the Britons' reigned at Camulodunum, where all his gold coins were struck. His coin designs were strongly classicising and rationalising, the remnants of Apollo's wreath, for example, being interpreted as an ear of corn on this gold stater. By the end of his long reign, about AD 40, he seems to have subdued most of south-east England.

(Captions by courtesy of Dr John Kent.)

2 Walmer Beach: the suggested landing place of Julius Caesar. The chalk cliffs can be seen rising towards the South Foreland in the background

3

The first formal Roman contact with Britain could hardly be rated an outstanding success. Indeed, so certain were the British tribes that Caesar would not return, that only two sent the correct, stipulated quota of hostages to Gaul, while the remainder altogether ignored the demand. The expedition was probably only rescued from complete disaster by the quality of Caesar's generalship; a lesser man might have been closer to total failure. Yet it had one important result. It

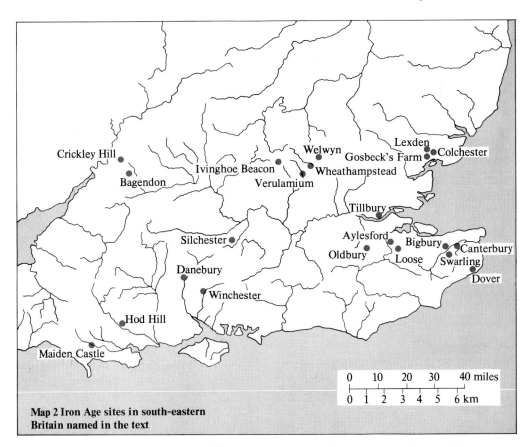

**Map 2 Iron Age sites in south-eastern Britain named in the text**

focused Roman interest on Britain and, though Caesar had been acting strictly beyond his authority as a provincial governor in mounting the invasion, it brought him official thanks from the Senate, and gained approval for further action.

Almost immediately on return to Gaul, preparations were started for the next year's campaign. Special transports, of dimensions more suitable for amphibious warfare, were ordered, and some 600 had been constructed by the following spring, in addition to an increased number of warships. But, as before, renewed hostilities in northern Gaul caused delays, and it was not until early July that the invasion fleet could sail. The combined force included five legions and some 2,000 cavalry, and it took with it many baggage animals, and large quantities of supplies. It was, altogether, a better-equipped and organised expedition, and more attention was paid to logistics.

It seems that, after an uneventful crossing, an unopposed landing was made on the same part of the Kentish coast as

had previously served as a beach-head. By making use of speed and surprise tactics, Caesar was able to march inland, cross a river, supposedly the river Stour, and capture the first major fortified place that he came to, usually identified as the hill-fort at Bigbury. Once more, though, his rapid progress inland was interrupted by a storm which drove ashore many of the ships anchored in the Channel. Despite his customary vigour, ten days were lost in setting matters right, during which time the whole fleet was beached above the reach of the tides and within a fortified area. In view of his previous experience, it is surprising that this had not been done at once.

The pause in the campaign had, however, allowed a regrouping of the British forces under a paramount leader, Cassivellaunus, who, ruling north of the Thames, was probably king of the tribe who later emerge as the Catuvellauni. An army, collected from many parts of Britain was, consequently, ready and waiting for Caesar on his next approach to the river crossing. There followed a series of running engagements, in which the Britons made maximum use of their war chariots to cause confusion among the Romans, who were unused to such methods of fighting. Ultimately, however, Caesar successfully defeated the Britons, after a large detachment of his army had been attacked while foraging. The Britons were then pursued by the whole cavalry force and fled in disorder. The march to the Thames followed; Caesar crossed by a ford, which had been fortified by

3 (*left*) The north-eastern rampart of Bigbury, near Canterbury, Kent, supposedly the scene of one of Caesar's major battles

4 (*right*) The northern rampart at Bigbury under excavation in 1978

5

the Britons, and which is located, by varying opinions, somewhere between Brentford and London, although the most recently expressed view favours a crossing in the neighbourhood of Tilbury. Certainly, Caesar very soon found himself in Trinovantian territory, which largely equates with modern Essex, so that one of the more easterly crossing points is best accepted.

Cassivellaunus still managed to maintain his pressure on the Roman army by using guerrilla tactics in the thickly-wooded areas north of the Thames. The same forests also helped to conceal his stronghold, while, in order to make the Roman army's advance still more difficult, he withdrew the inhabitants of the area, together with all animals and food stocks, so making it almost impossible for Caesar to obtain information or provisions.

But the British alliance, already under pressure, wavered and collapsed. First to make peace were the Trinovantes, who had previously suffered from Cassivellaunian aggression. In return for supplying hostages and food, they were thus saved from attack both by the Roman army and by their western neighbours. Other tribes joined in submitting to Caesar, and, among other gains, provided him with vital information concerning the position of Cassivellaunus' *oppidum,* protected, as he described, 'by forests and marshes' and 'filled with a large number of cattle'. Caesar assaulted it on two sides simultaneously and, despite its excellent fortifications and great natural strength, it was quickly captured. It has been argued for a long time that the site of the *oppidum* lay at Wheathampstead in Hertfordshire.

Caesar's capture of Cassivellaunus' stronghold did not, however, end the war. The latter, apparently a resourceful foe, organised an uprising in Kent, during which the Roman beach-head base was attacked, but without much success, whereupon he sued for peace, invoking the help of Commius, a Gaulish king and Caesar's ally and friend. By now also, the Roman army's campaigning season was nearing its close and Caesar decided to withdraw across the Channel before the onset of winter, partly fearing another rebellion in Gaul. Hostages were accepted, a tribute was fixed, and Cassivellaunus' tribe was forbidden further to interfere in Trinovantian affairs. Finally Caesar returned to Gaul by about mid-September, thus ending his second, more successful expedition to Britain. Whether he ever intended to return is arguable; but, if he had intentions so to do, they were upset by a series of revolts in Gaul, in late 54 BC and again in 53 BC. Thereafter he needed to direct his

attentions eastwards across the Rhine. Indeed, settlement
of the Gaulish problem did not come about until 51 BC, after
which matters of greater weight in Rome itself were to
engage his attention to the exclusion of all else.

Such is the basic outline of the Caesarian narrative and its
orthodox interpretation; on the whole, archaeology can con-
tribute little more to it. Geographical positions are but
sketchily described and often difficult to identify with accu-

racy, and the short span of time during which Caesar was in
Britain must mean that only the most ephemeral traces of
the Roman army's presence will have been left behind. Yet,
it is perhaps surprising that no evidence for the campaign
camps or other fortifications have come to light, until it is
remembered that little more is known of the early stages of
the later Roman invasion in AD 43. But, in places, there
must exist, perhaps somewhere in the region of Walmer,
again near Canterbury, and again at a point along the banks
of the Thames, as well as in Hertfordshire or Essex and
elsewhere, traces of the fortifications described by Caesar
as having been erected by his army. The army suffered
casualties, so cemeteries must equally exist, with the likely

5 Aerial photograph of the
*oppidum* at Wheathampstead
from the south-east. The
principal dykes are marked by
the two main belts of trees

possibility that they contained military equipment. It is not entirely due to want of looking that they have not been found, and it is unfortunate that many of the areas in question are, today, built over. It is strange, nevertheless, that no object or structure has yet been discovered that can, with confidence, be attributed to the campaigns of Caesar. Such a lack might suggest that it is time for a reappraisal of accepted theories.

To begin with, it is not easy to place the position of his original landing-place far from Walmer, owing to the way in which he describes the coastal topography of the neighbourhood. Admittedly there are other places along the Kentish coast where similar configurations occur, but to adopt one or more of them would place excessive and unacceptable strains on the remaining evidence, such as the duration of his crossing and the direction of the currents. Neither is it easy to postulate any place other than Bigbury, near Canterbury, for the fortified site some twelve miles inland which he attacked, after a night march on his second expedition. Indeed, in a direct line, the distance from Walmer to the hills overlooking the valley of the river Stour at Canterbury is almost exactly thirteen English miles, and it may have been from these hills that he obtained his first view of the enemy's army. Caesar himself records that Bigbury was taken by the well-tried Roman army method of making ramps to the top of the fortifications. Traces of such operations should be detectable by excavation, even if, following the Roman army's departure, they were removed. Unfortunately Bigbury has never been fully explored but, lying today in freshly-cleared woodland, and not far from the proposed line of the Canterbury by-pass the opportunity still exists and is now being undertaken.

There is, however, one alternative to Bigbury, which is worth considering. Twelve Roman miles (approximately 11¼ English miles) is the precise, straight-line distance from Walmer to the river Little Stour at Littlebourne. The topography of the ground beyond Littlebourne is similar to that across the Stour at Canterbury, and is, today, still heavily wooded. A fortified settlement of late Iron Age date has also been observed during gravel-quarrying in the area. Unfortunately little is known about it, and it would be unwise to speculate further, but it should be remembered when such theories are discussed.

Caesar's crossing of the Thames has already been considered, but little has yet been said of the Cassivellaunian kingdom and stronghold, apart from mentioning that it is usually placed at Wheathampstead.

Caesar's narrative does not, in fact, mention the Catuvellauni by name, but simply places Cassivellaunus' kingdom adjacent to the Trinovantes, and it would be unreasonable, and it would also introduce an unnecessary complication, to suppose that Cassivellaunus ruled any other tribe. For many years the Catuvellauni have usually been described as of Belgic origin, associated with the possible parent tribe of the Catalauni of northern Gaul, but more recently doubts have been cast on this attribution, and it may be that they were one of the 'indigenous', non-Belgic tribes mentioned by Caesar; their origin is discussed more fully below. Be that as it may, their ruler Cassivellaunus, a warlike and aggressive leader, must be seen as one of the strongest personalities in Britain at the time of the Roman expeditions, since he was given paramountcy over the other tribes.

Where then was Cassivellaunus' stronghold, protected by 'forests and marshes'? Ever since Mortimer Wheeler's excavations in the 1930s, Wheathampstead has been the first claimant, but more recent views have doubted the confidence of this assertion. Indeed, one modern authority even questions the existence of an *oppidum* at Wheathampstead at all. Another favours Wallbury Camp, near Great Hallingbury (Essex), which must have lain near the Catuvellaunian-Trinovantian border. It can be readily appreciated, therefore, that much still remains to be learned of Caesar's campaigns, and that primary archaeological evidence is lacking everywhere.

What, however, of the country to which Caesar came and of which he gives some description of the nature and the people? He records that the island was approximately triangular in shape with the corner forming Kent pointing towards Gaul. He observed that the nights, during his stay, were shorter than on the European mainland; moreover, he was told of more distant islands, which, in mid-winter, were in perpetual darkness. He also refers to Ireland and the Isle of Man. Iron was apparently found near the coast, almost certainly implying native knowledge of the ore deposits in the Weald of Kent and Sussex. A reference to tin 'from inland' can only be applied to that from Cornish sources, already known in the ancient world of the Mediterranean. Moreover, if, as he says, tin was known, it is surprising that copper had, seemingly, to be imported into southern Britain, for the two metals often occur together in Cornwall. Neither does he mention gold, silver or lead, although Mendip sources for the latter were being utilised in the Iron Age in the lake villages of Somerset. It would seem, therefore, that his information was, to some extent, restricted, and he does not appear to have become informed of all matters relating to the British economy.

On the agricultural side, he refers to the abundance of cattle and the numerous farms, remarking that the latter closely resemble those of Gaul. By implication, the farmers in the south-east clearly grew cereals, in comparison with the inland tribes. The country which he saw was also heavily populated, but its natural appearance must have been

**6** The Devil's Dyke, Wheathampstead

affected by the absence, so he says, of two types of trees: beech and fir. Remembering how common the beech is today on the chalk downlands of the south-east, it would be interesting to know the composition of the woods which Caesar frequently mentions in Kent and Hertfordshire; presumably oak predominated.

The most civilised people were recorded as living in Kent, and, since they must have been among the most recent immigrants from Gaul, it is not surprising that he saw a strong resemblance in their way of life. What is more surprising is that the same accolade is not accorded the people of Essex, whose origins were apparently remarkably similar. It may be that Caesar obtained no first-hand knowledge of that area, as he had done for Kent. All are quoted as using woad, wearing their hair long, but shaving all their bodies bar their heads and lips. The popular picture of the early Celt as moustachioed, long-haired and blue-painted is, there-fore, derived from Caesar's description of them, and may not be too inaccurate. Polygamy was, seemingly, also practised by family groups.

It would appear that, when compared with the modern archaeological evidence, Caesar's account, although bald and lacking in much circumstantial detail, is basically accu-rate. Admittedly for some time past the Catuvellauni were normally thought to have been of Belgic origin, but more recent views have, as indicated above, relegated them to the indigenous stock described by Caesar. So we can see that the Britain, to which Caesar came in 55 BC, had already been subjected to settlement by Belgic peoples from northern Gaul, and the clue to the areas so settled is pro-vided by a study of the typical artefacts which they brought with them.

## Chapter two

**Power politics –**

The movements of Belgic people to Britain, referred to at the end of the preceding chapter, began in the second century BC, and at first affected the coastal areas of eastern England, such as north and east Kent, Essex and the lower Thames valley. Two coin types can be distinguished at this time and their distributions are to some extent complementary to one another, suggesting the existence of at least two political orientations. Further Belgic migrations are indicated by later, successive coin sequences, and at one stage, some time before Caesar's arrival, they lend support to the undeniable link, which, as he mentioned, existed between parts of Britain and the ruler Diviciacus of the Gallic tribe of Suessiones. Consequently, by the time Caesar reached Britain, the main areas of Belgic settlement appear to have reached in an arc from the Essex coast northwards round to the middle Thames, across east and north Kent into Surrey, and with more minor settlements along the coastal plain of Sussex. For the remaining areas of Britain much, including parts of the south-west, the East Midlands and Yorkshire, continued under the domination of Iron B, or Marnian, groups, while the rest, chiefly in the highland zones, was still in a state owing much to Iron A, or even to earlier Late Bronze Age cultures.

What then of the Catuvellauni? It is important that we should obtain the right answer to this question, as it was their existence and attitudes which largely governed Rome's actions towards Britain. But for them, Britain might not have become a Roman province.

As already indicated in the previous chapter, the Catuvellauni had for long been assumed by archaeologists to be of Belgic origin, with tribal centres, first at Wheathampstead, second at Verulamium and last at Camulodunum (Colchester), in the tribal territory of the Trinovantes. But these conclusions have been closely questioned in recent years, leading to a complete reassessment of the interpretations. Indeed, one aspect of the earlier assumptions immediately stands out from all the rest, and, although noted, has not until the last few years received the emphasis it deserved. Caesar was extremely surprised when he was

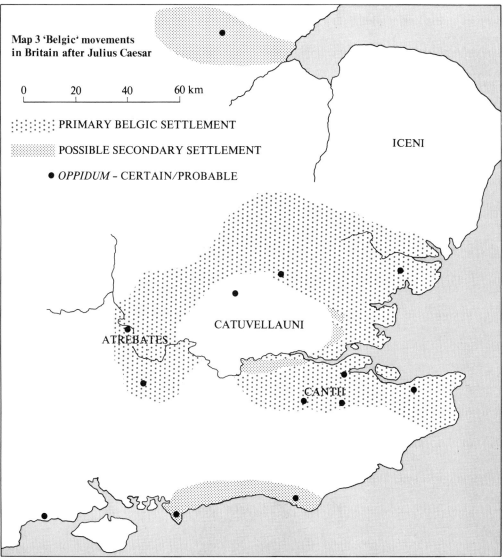

Map 3 'Belgic' movements
in Britain after Julius Caesar

0    20    40    60 km

:::::::: PRIMARY BELGIC SETTLEMENT

POSSIBLE SECONDARY SETTLEMENT

● *OPPIDUM* – CERTAIN/PROBABLE

ICENI

CATUVELLAUNI

ATREBATES

CANTII

opposed by a large body of war-chariots in the army of
Cassivellaunus, because such methods of fighting had long
since ceased to be used on the continental mainland. It
would be unlikely, therefore, if this form of warfare had
been introduced by any of the Belgic tribes who arrived
before Caesar's expeditions. That being so, its retention in
Britain probably descended through one or more groups,
whose ancestry lay in the Marnian migrations of a century or
so before. When other evidence is considered in conjunction
with this suggestion, it is difficult to avoid the conclusion
that it was Cassivellaunus' tribe who were responsible,
especially since he, as the supreme commander of the

13

British forces, appears to have placed great store by his chariots and was clearly accustomed to their management in war.

When we come to consider the tribal area which was ruled by Cassivellaunus, we must turn primarily to the numismatic and archaeological evidence. Most coinage found in Britain dating to the early years of Belgic penetration was minted in Gaul and carried across by the migrants. Conse-

7 Aerial photograph of the earthworks of the *oppidum* at Prae Wood, St Albans

quently a number of different coin styles can be identified and related to successive movements of tribes. Two, in particular, are important for our present arguments: Gallo-Belgic C and Gallo-Belgic E. The former appear to be related to the Gaulish Suessiones, whose ruler, Diviciacus, appears to have controlled tracts of land in both Britain and Gaul. Although their distribution in Britain is somewhat limited, the coins enjoyed a considerable influence, giving rise to several series of British-produced coins including, ultimately, a type known as British L (see Plate 1).

Gallo-Belgic E coins have, by comparison, a much wider distribution over south-east Britain, and, despite the fact that it is difficult to ascribe them to a particular tribal movement or ruler they are normally dated to the period just preceding Caesar's first expedition in 55. Yet, in their distribution, there exists a noticeable gap between the Thames and the Chilterns, covering southern Essex, Middlesex and Hertfordshire and it seems likely that we can fit the kingdom of Cassivellaunus into this hiatus, while at the same time we can possibly attribute to him the locally-produced British L series of coins.

Having placed Cassivellaunus' kingdom in the Hertfordshire region, it is again difficult to avoid the conclusion that

8 Aerial photograph showing crop-marks in the Sheepen Farm area of the *oppidum* at Colchester

it was the Catuvellauni over whom he ruled, for they appear there in later periods and there is hardly room for two tribes. Moreover, if Cassivellaunus and his people were descended from Marnian immigrants, it would explain the antipathy which they appear to have felt for the more recently-arrived people of Belgic stock, settling first in north Essex, which may then have belonged to the Catuvellauni, and later extending their influence in a wide arc westwards, until the Catuvellaunian lands were almost completely encircled. That they were only encircled and not submerged is a good indicator of their tribal strength. Antipathy or no, it did not prevent an alliance being made by the two antagonists against the seemingly far greater threat of the Caesarian expeditions. But, as we have seen, the alliance soon fell apart, with the Trinovantes making a separate peace with the Romans and, by so doing, hoping perhaps to turn the tables on the Catuvellauni. Certainly, also, the Trinovantes would possibly have had more in common with Rome than with their western neighbour.

One further factor appears to support the suggestion that the Catuvellauni were not of Belgic stock. The large fortified settlements which were constructed under their aegis at Wheathampstead, Verulamium, and Camulodunum (Colchester) and later, possibly under their influence, at

15

Power politics –

Bagendon, Minchinhampton and Stanwick, consisted of large linear dykes, constructed so as to link together natural obstacles such as marsh or forest. They enclosed considerable areas, and it seems that they were primarily built to prevent infiltration by chariots. Indeed, this form of protection would be ideal against a mobile enemy, and was used extensively in Britain in 1940. For many years, these *oppida*, as they were called by Caesar and other contemporary

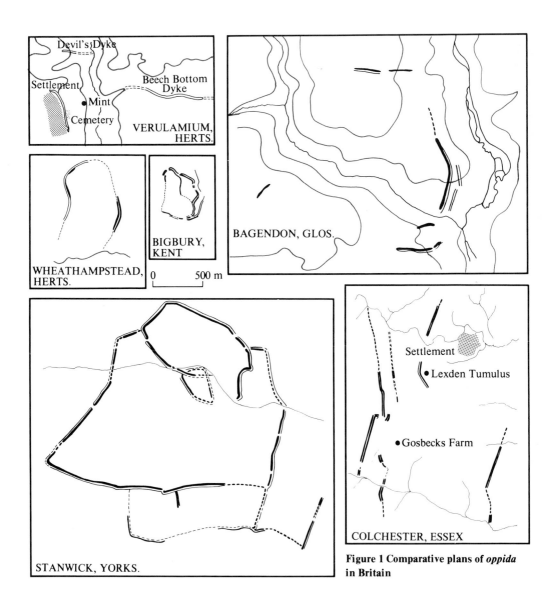

**Figure 1 Comparative plans of *oppida* in Britain**

authors, were attributed to Belgic tribes, but it can now be seen that, like the form of attack they were intended to prevent, they were archaic when compared with continental fortifications of the Caesarian period. They must, therefore, take their place with other Marnian-derived methods of defence, such as the multivallate hill-fort, being but a development of the latter which had been adapted to less undulating terrain and to a change in the methods of attack.

The fact that they continued to be built or perfected until well into the Roman period in Britain (i.e. Stanwick) despite the apparent ease with which the Roman army could overrun them, shows in this respect, if not in others, the essentially conservative nature of the tribe.

If this type of fortified enclosure is no longer considered to be Belgic, it remains to be seen what works were characteristic of these people. It seems likely that the reconstruction of some hill-fort ramparts and ditches, as at Oldbury (Kent), to give a profile in which the front slope of the bank is continuous with that of the inner face of a large, wide-bottomed ditch, belonged to the Belgic phase of the Iron Age. The type is usually named after the hill-fort at Fécamp in Seine Inférieure, and the form of construction would have been more capable of resisting attack by Roman siege engines.

Having placed the Catuvellauni in their correct context with respect to the Belgic immigrants, it remains to consider the political developments which took place in Britain following Caesar's expeditions.

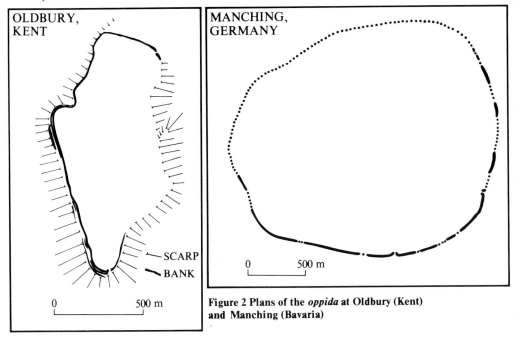

Figure 2 Plans of the *oppida* at Oldbury (Kent) and Manching (Bavaria)

10 Statue of Vercingetorix, erected at Alesia in 1865

As already indicated in the previous chapter, Caesar imposed terms on the British tribes on his departure. Cassivellaunus was forbidden to molest his eastern neighbour, while payment of tribute was fixed and hostages taken to ensure that the terms of the treaties were observed. The alliance which Rome forged with the Trinovantes seems, moreover, to have led to increased trade with Gaul, especially in wine, for imported amphorae, or wine jars, are now found in their territory in increasing numbers, and the distribution of these vessels helps to delimit the tribal area.

A further major upheaval occurred some five years after Caesar's expeditions. Commius, his one-time ally and friend, threw in his lot with another Gaulish leader, Vercingetorix, during the great rebellion of 52 BC, and was ultimately forced to flee to Britain, whither he came with a considerable following, having declared his intention of never setting eyes on a Roman again. The distribution of Commian coins suggests that he established a kingdom in west Sussex and east Hampshire, an area where he may already have had links with earlier settlers, and which eventually seems to have been expanded northwards to occupy the middle Thames region.

During the next twenty years or so, it is difficult to trace

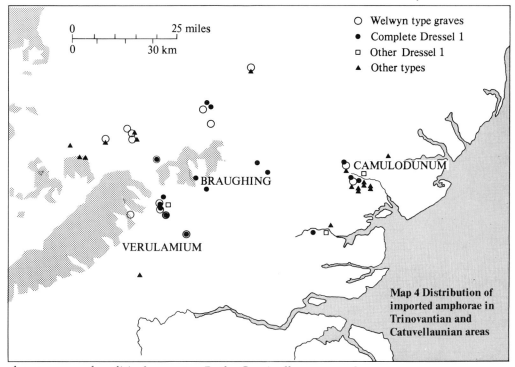

0    25 miles

0    30 km

○ Welwyn type graves
● Complete Dressel 1
□ Other Dressel 1
▲ Other types

CAMULODUNUM

BRAUGHING

VERULAMIUM

**Map 4 Distribution of imported amphorae in Trinovantian and Catuvellaunian areas**

the course of political events. Both Cassivellaunus and Commius duly died to be succeeded by Tasciovanus and Tincommius respectively. Tasciovanus, possibly the son, or more likely the grandson, of Cassivellaunus, was the first Catuvellaunian ruler to issue coins inscribed with his name, and with a mint-mark, which clearly showed the removal of the tribal capital to Verulamium. Possibly also, and contrary to the terms of the earlier Caesarian treaty, he seems to have renewed the pressure against the Trinovantes, even for a brief time, perhaps, occupying their capital at Camulodunum. Augustus was, by now, emperor in Rome, and a timely visit to Gaul, where among other things a defeat of the Roman army on the Rhine had to be attended to, may have led to the Catuvellaunian withdrawal from the territory of a tribe still ostensibly in treaty relations with Rome.

In Hampshire and Sussex, Tincommius overcame the aversion shown by his father, Commius, to Rome, not entirely with the wholehearted approval of his supporters. It may, indeed, have been this decision which caused a breakaway movement of part of the tribe towards the upper Thames valley and into Gloucestershire to form the tribe of the Dobunni. Nevertheless, diplomatic initiatives ensued

19

between Tincommius and Augustus with a formal treaty the probable outcome. So we might infer from the sudden emergence of a coin series closely resembling Roman styles, and probably introduced with the technical help of Roman craftsmen. It is at this point that we can begin to detect the statecraft of Augustus, who had, on at least two previous occasions, apparently considered further expeditions to Britain, only for each to prove abortive because of other

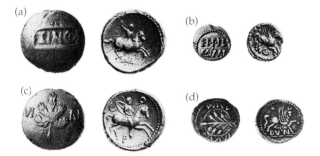

**11** Coins: (a) *Tincommius* (Mack no.96). His coins name him 'son of Commius'. An imitative silver type shows that he was reigning after about 12 BC, but before the end of Augustus' reign in AD 14, the Monumentum Ancyranum declares that he had fled suppliant to the emperor. His coins span the transition from types based on Celtic proto-types to designs almost wholly of classical inspiration.

(b) *Eppillus* (Mack no.302). The rare coins of this 'son of Commius' are of two styles; some, with bold Roman letters, proclaim him 'King of Calleva', the others (as illustrated), of a blander style, come at least in part from Kent.

(c) *Verica* (Mack no.125). This third 'son of Commius' also used more than one mint, including that of Calleva. His later coins, with the vine-leaf motif, must be related to the corn-ear design of Cunobelinus (see Plate 1 (f)) and he is readily identifiable with the Berichos, refugee at the court of Caligula. The distribution of the coins of his contemporary and rival Cunobelinus extends far into the area formerly dominated by issues of the family of Commius.

(d) *Amminus* (Mack no.313). He has been plausibly identi-fied with Adminius, a son of Cunobelinus expelled from Britain by his father. Perhaps he was an under-king, perhaps just a rebel. DVN on this silver coin presumably denotes the place of mintage, but might be a patronymic, if he were not in fact the son of Cunobelinus. His coinage might be Kentish, but this is not certain.

(Captions by courtesy of Dr John Kent.)

more urgent distractions. The treaty with Tincommius now gave him a foothold in Britain which could be maintained without the necessity for direct military intervention. He probably recognised the danger of uncontrolled Catuvel-launian expansion to the east and south coasts and the inability of the Trinovantes to resist it on their own. Conse-quently a friendly state situated between the Thames and the south coast would have helped to neutralise the threat, and would have acted as a suitable buffer. It was, therefore, in Augustus' interest to maintain a balance of power in Britain with the tacitly anti-Roman Catuvellauni being countered by his new ally.

Tincommius, however, fared badly and was the victim of a plot by his own brothers, Eppillus and Verica. He fled to Rome where he no doubt hoped to gain the help of Augustus for his reinstatement. His request was refused; in a pragmatic decision, made in order to perpetuate the British arrangements, Augustus recognised first one and then the other of his two brothers and in addition probably accorded them the title Rex, implying the status of client kings. Unfortunately fraternal strife did not cease with the ousting of Tincommius. Eppillus was soon to follow and, after his expulsion, seems to have moved to Kent, where he, in turn, ejected the king Dubnovellaunos. Not to be out-done, the latter may have moved to Essex, where the throne was possibly vacant following the death of Addedomaros, and so assumed the kingship of the Trinovantes. As so often happened in Belgic politics, a single action was often followed by numerous repercussions, and Verica's successful attempt to gain the sole rule of Tincommius' Atrebatic realm is just such a case, which fortunately can be followed by an examination of the relevant coins and their distributions.

Meanwhile, Tasciovanus was quietly pursuing a policy of expansion. Denied by the threat of Roman intervention from annexing the Trinovantian kingdom, he pushed northwards into the southern midlands and possibly also into

12 Medallion of Augustus found in the Lexden tumulus, Colchester

west Kent, before dying, seemingly, in the first decade of the first century AD, leaving, so it has been suggested, his kingdom in a state of disorder.

The next main move to be observed is the appearance at Camulodunum, the capital of the Trinovantes, of the monarch Cunobelin, who on certain of his coins styles himself as the son of Tasciovanus. Opinion is sharply divided on this attribution. The more orthodox explanations accept it at its face value, and conclude, therefore, that Cunobelin, son of Tasciovanus, had, just before his father's death, at last risked Roman wrath to overcome the Trinovantes and had, moreover, planted his capital on theirs. Such an action would probably imply that Tasciovanus was still ruling from the Catuvellaunian centre at Verulamium, so that Cunobelin had to depend on his own resourcefulness until after his father's death, when his new capital could become the principal tribal centre at the same time as he became supreme monarch. Recently, however, an alternative suggestion has been put forward. Cunobelin has been seen as a Trinovantian nobleman, who wrested the

21

kingship from Dubnovellaunos and conquered the Catuvellauni. In order to confuse the defeated tribe, he subscribed to a piece of pure propaganda and claimed to be the son of their deceased ruler, Tasciovanus. Yet to accept this alternative places a considerable strain on other evidence. In the first place it would be difficult to account for the complete turnabout in Trinovantian politics and feelings towards the Romans which such action would represent, not so much during Cunobelin's reign, but after his death. It is hard to accept also the sudden reversal which must have occurred in the relative strengths of the two tribes, even if Caesar describes the Trinovantes as one of the strongest in Britain. Even greater difficulty arises at the time of the Roman invasion of AD 43, when, by implication, the chief enemy in Britain is clearly the Catuvellauni. It would be strange, indeed, if Cunobelin, a Trinovantian by birth, had abandoned the use of the name of his own tribe in favour of one which he had conquered.

It is probably best, therefore, to retain the orthodox interpretation and conclude that Cunobelin's claim to be the son of Tasciovanus was correct, that he had at last managed to do what the Catuvellauni had been attempting for years and that he had recovered the territory lost to the Trinovantes in the pre-Caesarian period by their complete subjugation. He was clearly a powerful man, who remained the dominant personality in Britain for nearly forty years, even being styled King of the Britons by a classical author. Conquest of the Trinovantes would have been well within his scope. It was a bold act and would, almost certainly, have led to a flurry of diplomatic protests by both the Trinovantes and Augustus. Nevertheless, it is likely that Cunobelin had picked the right moment, for in AD 9 Roman arms suffered a serious disaster in Germany, when an expeditionary force consisting of three legions was annihilated in the Teutoberger forest: Augustus was in no position to take military action in Britain, a decisive factor probably well known to Cunobelin.

Yet if Cunobelin's reign started so inauspiciously for the Romans, efforts were later made at recovery. Soon after Augustus' death, it is recorded that certain British rulers, among whom Cunobelin may be included, sent embassies to Rome and even made offerings in the Capitol. At one stage, Cunobelin is even styling himself as Rex on his coins, which implies a degree of Roman acceptance, while trade connections between his kingdom and the Roman empire appear to have been assiduously fostered, if the wealth of imported material at Camulodunum is considered. More-

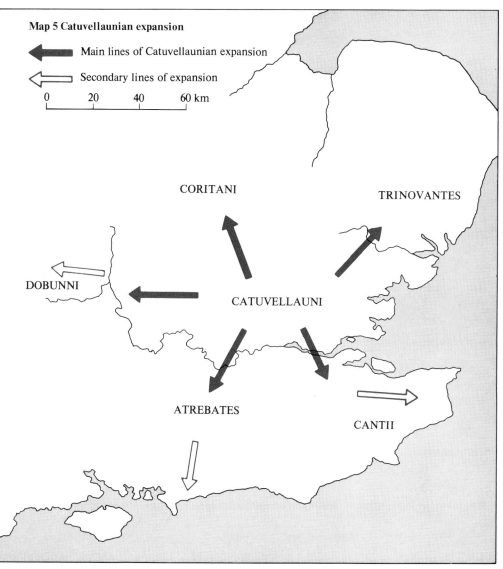

**Map 5 Catuvellaunian expansion**

Main lines of Catuvellaunian expansion

Secondary lines of expansion

0   20   40   60 km

CORITANI

TRINOVANTES

DOBUNNI

CATUVELLAUNI

ATREBATES

CANTII

over, further expansion of the Catuvellaunian empire into east Kent and into the northern part of the Atrebatic client kingdom, where Epaticcus, Cunobelin's brother, had installed himself at Silchester, appears to have taken place without serious protest from Rome although the latter move must have called for some remonstrance.

Admittedly the policy of Tiberius, who had become emperor on the death of Augustus, was somewhat different. We are told that he avoided foreign entanglements as far as possible and attempted to follow the injunction laid down by Augustus not to expand the empire further. So long as Verica remained ruler of the Atrebates and pro-

Power politics –

Roman in outlook, and so long as Cunobelin remained well-disposed to Rome, the theoretical balance of power in Britain seemed to be maintained and there was no good reason for military action.

Cunobelin seems to have limited his territorial expansion to the areas mentioned above, although it is quite clear that his influence extended well beyond his boundaries, and, in so far as his kingdom and that of Verica were concerned and

**13** Coins: (a) *Dubnovellaunus* (Mack no.275) and (b) *Atthedomarus* (=*Addedomaros*) (Mack no. 266). These rulers are generally held to be Trinovantian, but the distribution of their coins does not differ fundamentally from that of Tasciovanus and Cunobelinus. The relationship of these groups of coinage remains to be elucidated. We cannot be sure that this Dubnovellaunus was identical with the one who ruled in Kent, or with the Dumnovellaunus who fled to Augustus. The inscriptions of Atthedomarus ('Big Spear') are remarkable for the use of DD and the Greek Θ to denote the aspirate, long lost in Latin.
(c) *Corio* . . . (Mack no.393) and (d) *Bodvoc* (Mack no.395). These were rulers of the Dobunni. The coins of the latter are typologically the later, and presumably date to the time of the Claudian invasion. The staters of Corio . . . are more conservative, and may be a little earlier, though the obverse is clearly modelled on Cunobelinus' corn-ear. The two series have quite distinct distributions within Dobunnic territory, and it has been supposed that they ruled over different parts of the one people.
(Captions by courtesy of Dr John Kent.)

their relations with Rome, Britain seems to have remained moderately stable for the next two or three decades. The volume of trade between Britain and the Roman empire grew, and the goods so introduced were also traded internally. Consequently imported pottery is to be found on a wide range of sites in the south in the years preceding the conquest.

There can be few doubts that Cunobelin was always more powerful than Verica, but so long as a degree of restraint was maintained little harm was done, and Cunobelin, so long as he retained full control, did so. Nevertheless, towards the end of his reign, we can begin to detect a hardening in attitudes, caused probably by a depreciation of his powers during his declining years, which was matched by the ascendency being gained by his sons, Togodumnus and Caratacus. In addition, pressure seems to have been resumed against Verica and the Atrebates, either by Epaticcus or his apparent successor at Silchester, Caratacus, so that by about AD 40 the kingdom was apparently reduced to a small area centred on Chichester and Selsey Bill and marked by a series of dykes. At about the same time a thrust was made up the Thames Valley, far into Dobunnian territory. In the wedge so created a puppet, or Quisling, king named Boduoccus was placed, with a possible capital at Minchinhampton, near Stroud. To north and south, the Dobunnian monarch Corio . . ., continued to rule his sundered kingdom.

On the northern frontier of the Catuvellauni, attempts

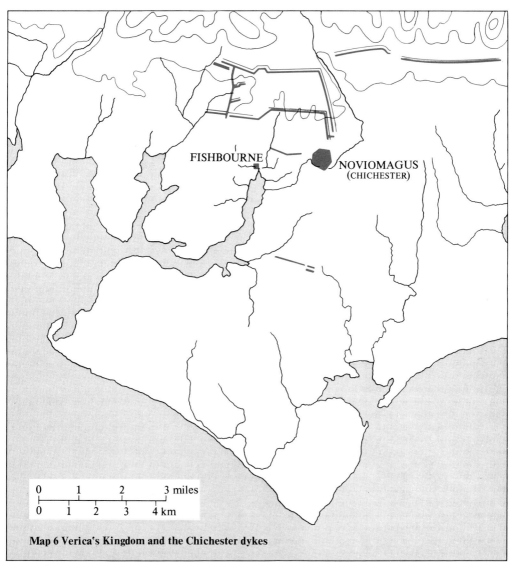

FISHBOURNE

NOVIOMAGUS
(CHICHESTER)

0     1     2     3 miles

0   1   2   3   4 km

**Map 6 Verica's Kingdom and the Chichester dykes**

were also being made to expand into Icenian territory in
Norfolk. It is evident, however, that though a little progress
was made, the Iceni seem to have been more successful in
resisting and only marginal changes took place. The same
may be true of their other neighbours to the north-west, the
Coritani, who, although apparently ruled by a Belgic
dynasty, appear to have kept their independence.

The increasing power of Cunobelin's two more impetuous sons was demonstrated yet again within his lifetime, for in AD 40 they expelled, presumably with their
father's approval, their brother Adminius. Since he fled to
Rome, it is likely that he incurred their displeasure by too

25

open a display of pro-Roman feelings and attitudes. From the distribution of his few coins we may conclude that his area of influence lay in Kent, although after the conquest he may have returned to Verulamium, occupying the sometime Catuvellaunian capital. On arrival in Rome he petitioned Gaius Caligula, Tiberius' successor, for help in recovering his position, representing to him the ease with which he could invade and capture Britain. Gaius was at that time in Germany where he had been engaged in suppressing a revolt. Swayed by the arguments of Adminius, he collected an army at Boulogne ready for the crossing, when mutiny broke out. His feeble mind was just as easily switched to the other extreme by this event, and the whole expedition was promptly called off, the magnificent lighthouse which he built at Boulogne being the only lasting reminder of it.

Shortly after, Cunobelin died and all restraining influences were now removed from the intemperate behaviour of his two sons. The surviving fragment of the Atrebatic kingdom was quickly annexed and the ageing Verica fled to Rome, to seek the aid of the emperor Claudius, who had succeeded Gaius upon the latter's murder. His expulsion was a more serious matter than had been the flight of earlier princes, such as Dubnovellaunos and Adminius. It represented a major insult to an ally and client of the Roman state, which, if it went unavenged, would have called into question a whole area of imperial policy. Moreover, for the first time in nearly sixty years, the balance in Britain had been totally upset and Rome now found herself facing a coastline across the Channel which was entirely in hostile hands, and which was controlled by a comparatively unified power whose boundaries stretched almost from the Wash in the north to the south coast and from Kent and Essex in the east to Hampshire and Gloucestershire in the west. Moreover, the enormity of the situation was compounded when a demand was made for Verica's extradition. With its refusal, disturbances were caused, either on the Gaulish coast, or in Britain, where the lives and property of numerous Roman merchants may have been threatened. Britain was by now a considerable market for the products of the western empire, and almost certainly an exporter of valuable raw materials; an interruption in the trade might have had serious repercussions, not least in the loss in revenue of customs duties on goods passing the frontiers. Action became imperative if Roman prestige and influence were not to suffer. Moreover, the political excuse now existed for an action which had been contemplated on several occasions ever since Julius Caesar had departed from Britain.

In the previous chapter the rulers of a largely tribal Britain were discussed within the context of their political affili- ations and leanings. What then of the people they ruled over: of their warfare, customs and beliefs: of their settle- ments, dwellings and farms, industries and arts?

Britain was, from about 1000 BC, part of the Celtic world which embraced Gaul and most of Central Europe. So, every new band of migrants reaching Britain from the conti- nent re-emphasised this link, while often bringing with it the latest developments in warfare, metal-working, art or religion. Hence we see the consecutive introduction of the

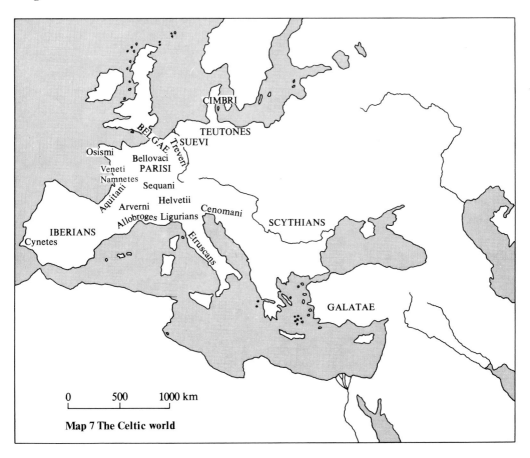

**Map 7 The Celtic world**

cultural life-styles which can be broadly summarised as Hallstatt and La Tène 1, 2 and 3, each of which tended to give rise to its own specifically British developments.

By the time Caesar arrived in Britain, much of the earlier Hallstatt culture in the south had been overlaid by, in turn, the early and middle La Tène styles, with which they in part fused to throw up a hybrid culture. Only in highland areas, especially in parts of Scotland, is it by then possible to find a

**14** The triumphal arch erected at Orange (Arausio) in Gallia Narbonensis, at about the time of the Caesarian campaigns, showing Celtic trophies below a scene illustrating nautical equipment

reasonably pure strain of Hallstatt culture surviving, but in a form adapted to different physical conditions.

It is, therefore, with the later La Tène that we are primarily concerned here, although it is important to remember the links that still existed with earlier periods and people. Moreover, since much of our account has so far dealt with both inter-tribal and external conflicts, it is probably appropriate to consider first the methods of Celtic warfare. In this it is

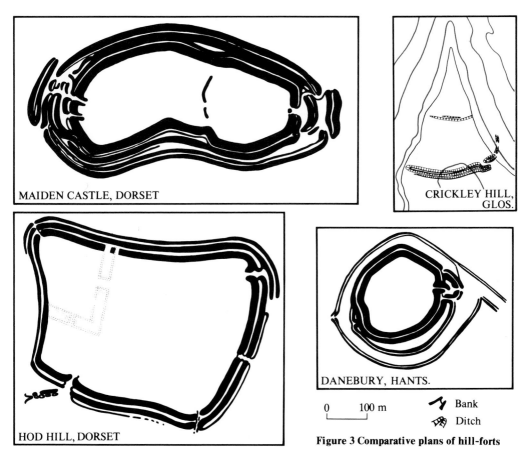

**Figure 3 Comparative plans of hill-forts**

unfortunate that most accounts of battles fought are derived from classical authors describing Celtic conflicts with the Roman army, and there is little information on inter-tribal disputes.

From the very beginning, the Celts placed great reliance on the construction of fortified enclosures for defence, with prominent hills being the most favoured sites. Often, at first, such places were defended only by a timber palisade, sometimes allied with an external ditch. But such fortifications were defective, in that they could easily be burnt to the ground, and so were soon replaced by more substantial works employing a variety of structural methods. In past decades, the construction of hill-forts in Britain was, without question, attributed by archaeologists to the Iron Age, but now with more excavation taking place and with better means available for establishing dates, it appears that a number predate the normal chronology given to the earliest Hallstatt immigrants by a considerable margin. In this re-

**15** Aerial photographs showing univallate hill-forts at (a) Ivinghoe Beacon (Bucks.); (b) Crickley Hill (Glos.)

spect the development pattern of fortifications in Britain can
be seen to match more closely that known for some time on
the continent. Ivinghoe Beacon, Crickley Hill, and Mam Tor
are but three examples where a Late Bronze Age date is most
appropriate.

Hill-forts, if classified by the character of their defences,
fall broadly into two main classes: univallate and multivallate, but there are many variations of type within these

categories, according to the nature of their entrances and the
methods of construction used in their ramparts. If considered in the most basic form, a hill-fort could be manufactured by simply digging a ditch around the top of a suitable
hill and piling the material from the excavation into a linear
mound inside the ditch, and this is, somewhat surprisingly,
the method employed in the very latest developments
during the Belgic, or late La Tène, period, after seemingly
more sophisticated and ingenious methods had been
abandoned. Admittedly as then constructed, the ditch was
both broader and often deeper than the earlier run of hill-
fort vallations, but nevertheless it was the most effective
form of defence against the war-engines of the Roman army.

In earlier periods, however, various methods were used
to support and contain the rampart material, while a different approach was again employed if the ditches were to

16 Rampart of the vitrified fort
at Abernethy (Perthshire)

31

be dug on a steep hillside. Combinations of vertical and horizontal timbering, sometimes, in suitable country, allied with dry-stone walling, were used to make a box-like rampart with vertical or near-vertical faces. The normal practice was to set vertical posts, either in individual pits, or in continuous trenches, at the front and rear and strap the two lines together with horizontal beams placed between them in the rampart core, so that the weight of material would not

**17** Aerial photographs showing multivallate hill-forts at (a) Badbury Rings (Dorset); (b) Eggardon (Dorset)

force the posts apart. These horizontal members were sometimes further strengthened by the addition of timbers set longitudinally across them. When combined with stone faces, these ramparts closely resembled the types observed by Caesar in Gaul, and hence called by him the *murus Gallicus*. The advantages of such ramparts are chiefly that a greater height can be achieved with a limited amount of material and that they provide vertical faces which must be scaled by any attacker. Its disadvantages were that, with the exception of the *murus Gallicus,* fire could weaken it, and that it was capable of being both undermined by tunnelling and broken by a battering ram.

It used to be thought that multivallate hill-forts were developed from the univallate variety, in order to neutralise the effect of a newly-introduced weapon, the sling, which was considered to have been brought to Britain by the Marnian immigrants of the early La Tène culture. No such certainty now remains, although hill-forts in some regions may have cultural associations. Indeed the introduction of multivallation may be seen perhaps as almost accidental if we consider fortifications which were constructed on a steep slope. Under such circumstances, considerable effort would be needed to cast the material from the ditch on to the uphill slope above, and it is usually found that the inner bank is constructed of material obtained from quarry pits or ditches in the interior, while that derived from the main ditch is disposed more easily on the downhill side as a counterscarp bank. There is then a strong similarity with a bivallate type of fortification, and it is only a short step on to true multivallation, in which more than one ditch is dug.

In any fortification, the weakest parts of the circuit are always at the gates. At first, hill-fort entrances were of simple construction and consisted of little more than timber gates set between the terminations of the rampart. But, as time passed, more and more complex structures appeared, leading to elaborately recessed passages into which an enemy could be enticed and then either cut off or attacked from both sides. Even more extreme were the tortuous entrances of Maiden Castle, or the projecting hornworks and central command post of the last reconstruction at Danebury.

The Celts were a warlike people, who seem, on occasion, to have decided battles by single combat between champions; yet no account of such engagement has been recorded by Roman sources and it must be admitted that this method of fighting was probably the exception rather than the rule. Great display was also made before battle was joined, and the superb workmanship of the bronzesmiths in manufacturing elaborately decorated shields, helmets, sword scabbards and horse-harness, was most likely intended to impress an enemy on just such an occasion. Pep-talks were also given, not only to hearten one's own side, but also to demoralise the enemy. The opening moves in any battle, therefore, contained much posturing and braggadocio in an attempt to create an atmosphere of confi-

**18** Gateway, in the course of excavation, of the hill-fort at Crickley Hill (Glos.)

dent success. Displays of armed might have always been a characteristic of aggressive peoples or nations and in this the La Tène Iron Age people of Britain and Europe were no different from Nazi Germany or modern Russia; all delight in trying to intimidate their enemies by suitable propaganda.

Once battle was joined, one of their methods of engaging an enemy was by the use of chariots, which were lightly constructed of wood and wickerwork and drawn mostly by a pair of ponies. The charioteers themselves were not armed and a warrior was not expected to fight from the vehicle. Instead they were used on the battlefield to impart a very high degree of mobility to the infantry. Caesar mentions the great skill of the charioteers, and although the vehicles were not intended for direct engagements, they would have had an extreme psychological effect on an enemy who was not prepared for them. In battle, each chariot with its driver could carry a warrior speedily into the very heart of the fight and, should the necessity arise, withdraw with him again almost as quickly. The only effective way of dealing with them, as Caesar found, was to use his cavalry in close conjunction with the infantry, and undoubtedly a force composed entirely of the latter was at a grave disadvantage, as they would have been unable to press home any initial successes which they may have won.

The Celtic forces in Britain which opposed Caesar, therefore, had a formidable weapon of highly mobile infantry, and it is recorded that Cassivellaunus disposed more than 4,000 chariots. This forms an interesting contrast with the means employed by Celtic people for static defence: the hill-fort and dyked enclosure. It has often been argued that the only part hill-forts could play in such warfare was to act as strongholds, from which mobile forces could emerge as necessary and fight or patrol in the surrounding areas. A defender, who by comparison, barricaded himself within the fortifications could do little to influence the outcome of a battle unless the enemy mounted a direct attack; otherwise the latter was free to roam at will doing as much damage as he could to crops, farms and settlements. Fortified enclosures, therefore, only made strategic sense when allied with an offensive, mobile army, who could fight outside them. Indeed the corollary is also true. The more mobile an army, the greater its need for secure places from which adequate back-up facilities can be provided to keep it in the field, and to supply it with fresh horses, fodder and new weapons to replace those lost or broken. Can we, therefore, see in places, such as Wessex, or the Welsh borders, with their multiplicity of hill-forts, not so much a political system suggestive of near anarchy with many petty chieftains each in his own stronghold, but a much more centralised and sophisticated system whereby the hill-forts provided numerous bases for a large chariot army? If so, it might well be the reason why not all hill-forts were permanently occupied, only needing to be commissioned in time of war.

The question whether or not hill-forts were permanently occupied has caused a good deal of discussion. It has been argued that the provision of guard-chambers at the gates, such as those at Rainsborough Camp, implies the presence of a regular garrison and so of an inhabited site. While many hill-forts, such as Hod Hill, Crickley Hill, Danebury and Ivinghoe Beacon, have produced evidence for internal structures some, equally, have not. Although this absence could be due to inadequate excavation, it seems unlikely to be the answer in every case. That being so, it is reasonable to suppose that those hill-forts which were not permanently inhabited were constructed to act solely as refuges for an outlying population in time of trouble. Naturally, though, most hill-forts, whether permanently occupied or not, will to some extent have so served.

The changes which took place, as recorded above, in the construction of fortifications during the later pre-Roman

**19** Aerial photograph of rectangular and circular timber buildings inside the hill-fort at Crickley Hill

Iron Age in Britain, were partly caused by the need to adapt to different political and settlement patterns and partly to take cognizance of new forms of warfare. The preference of Belgic tribes and people for lower-lying settlements meant that most hill-forts in the areas of their primary settlements were abandoned, or at any rate not reconstructed, in favour of fortified sites elsewhere. Occasionally, however, a hill-fort was refortified in the new style, as at Oldbury in Kent, with its massive dump rampart and wide ditch, which was attributed by its excavator to the eve of the Roman conquest. Moreover, the concentration of political power in fewer hands ultimately led to a reduction in the number of fortified centres, while the choice of valley-side or riverside sites denoted a strong desire on the part of the builders to control both river crossings and trade routes, many of which followed the courses of rivers. Such sites as Loose, near Maidstone, or Winchester must be included as typical of the valley-side sites so chosen, and their positions show them to be of almost pure Belgic origin.

Among these new-style fortifications must be included the great *oppida,* such as Camulodunum (Colchester). In these, considerable areas of ground were enclosed by a system of discontinuous multiple dykes. At Colchester, if we exclude the series around Gosbecks Farm which seem to form an earlier nucleus, no less than, in some places, three successive lines of formidable earthworks protected the core of the settlement at Sheepen, usually believed to be the capital of Cunobelin. The lines appear to run from river valley to river valley, and since they are largely absent east of the main centre, it is probably right to assume that on that side, the marshy and, perhaps, tidal estuaries of the river Coln and its tributaries provided the necessary protection. The whole position is, therefore, one of considerable strength, and we may be forgiven for wondering what might have happened if the armies of Togodumnus and Caratacus had been less impetuous and instead of attacking the Roman army in Kent, had lured them back to their fortress at Camulodunum. The combination of natural obstacles and massive dykes might well have provided a different outcome to the engagement.

If we are right in our assumption that Cunobelin was a direct lineal descendant of Marnian stock, who had defeated and taken control of the Belgic Trinovantes, then it is probably right also to assume that the defences of Camulodunum represent an amalgamation of the older style anti-chariot fortifications of his predecessors, as at Wheathampstead and Verulamium, with the more recently adapted styles of the Belgae, which were intended to resist assaults by the siege-engines of the Roman army. In this respect they would certainly have been initially successful since their dimensions would have been too great to allow the immediate access of such weapons and the banks, of dump construction, would have been proof against the normal engines of attack mounted by the Romans.

Comment has sometimes been made of the extremely insular quality of the late La Tène *oppida* of Britain. None exactly resemble the great sites of Gaul or central Europe, such as that at Manching in southern Germany, while one largely looks in vain on the continent for fortified enclosures such as Camulodunum. Our conclusion that this and similar sites may, therefore, represent a combination of early La Tène methods, specially adapted, in Britain, for chariot warfare, with those of the later La Tène anti-siege fortifications, may well be right. They should, perhaps in consequence, be considered as peculiarly British phenomena, and their wider distribution outside Catuvellaunian homelands, with similar sites occurring possibly at Minchinhampton in Gloucestershire, at Silchester and even as far north as Stanwick in north Yorkshire, may be seen as the extension of Catuvellaunian influence and power.

Besides the fortified enclosures of different types detailed above there were many other settlements of variable size, ranging from large villages to single farms and homesteads. Most would have depended on an agricultural economy, although there were a number situated in coastal areas such as round the Wash, the Thames and Severn estuaries, where the extraction of salt from sea water, coupled with fishing and the collection of shellfish, provided the mainstay; many oyster shells were found in a house of Belgic date at Canterbury, and indicate an exploitation of the local beds which were, within a few decades, to become of commercial importance. In many cases the settlements were contained in enclosures consisting of a low bank and small ditch; it is likely that the banks were sometimes surmounted by hedges although, in many cases, fences were erected not only to keep out wild animals and sneak-thieves but also more importantly, we might suspect, to keep stock and young children from straying. In the highland areas such as Cornwall, Wales and the north, stone walls often replaced fences.

Variations in settlement types and patterns can be detected in some places which probably indicate different cultural origins, and it would be foolish to expect a common pattern, even over lowland England, at any one time in the decades preceding the Roman invasion. The most commonly occurring type of settlement enclosure in the late Iron Age is undoubtedly that of sub-rectangular form; there is also a tendency for a greater degree of nucleation to take place following the Belgic migrations. Indeed it has been noted that, in those areas primarily affected by Belgic peoples, relatively few sites of earlier date show continuity into this period, and it is to be assumed that individual farms were being abandoned in favour of a more communal life often on new sites.

Most farms and settlements were associated with field systems. On hill slopes, especially in the chalk regions, individual fields were delineated by lynchets, which were caused by soil-creep after ploughing had taken place, so giving rise to the characteristic enhanced slope between one field and the next below it. Unfortunately, it is known that these fields, usually termed 'Celtic' fields, continued to be used during the Roman period, and it is not always possible to attribute a definite pre-Roman date to their lay-out. On more level ground, such as valley bottoms, field systems can also be detected, often by aerial photography. They were frequently more irregular in shape and size, a factor not always unrelated to the close proximity of rivers or streams. In some instances, the patchwork effect of numerous small fields, each of which seldom exceeded half a hectare in area, is replaced by much larger dyked enclosures, sometimes associated with smaller sub-rectangular or circular examples approached through funnel-like entrances. The larger are normally interpreted as ranches for sheep or cattle, which could have been rounded up when necessary, and corralled in the smaller. Few field systems of indisputable pre-Roman date are known in the highland areas of Britain, and it is usually assumed that little cultivation was carried on, agricultural activities being restricted to the raising of cattle, sheep and horses, which would graze on the open moorland.

A moderately heavy plough, with an iron share, was in use in Britain in the decades before the Roman invasion, but it is now thought unlikely that the plough with coulter and mould-board had by then been introduced. Nevertheless the heavier loams and clays of valley bottoms could be cultivated, leading to improved production of cereals. It is unlikely though that the indigenous light plough, which did little more than scratch the surface of the ground, had been entirely replaced, and it would have still remained suitable for the thinner and lighter soils overlying chalk, gravel or sand. Also, it is probable that more primitive methods of cultivation continued in use, even though the good, iron-bound digging spade was, like the most advanced plough, a Roman introduction. The principal crops grown were barley, a wheat called emmer, and a small bean. Another variety of wheat — spelt — was being introduced during the Iron Age and had the advantage that it matured better in a damp climate, and was also suitable for autumn sowing. Since both forms of wheat were bearded like barley, it is difficult to identify both the ear of grain featured so often on Cunobelin's coins, and the imitation ears made of silver which were included in a rich burial at Lexden just outside Colchester; it is often claimed from this evidence that the wealth of Cunobelin's kingdom was concentrated in the production of barley, although the representations could equally be wheat. To what extent fruit and vegetables were grown under cultivation is not known. There would have been such an abundance of wild varieties that it would probably have been unnecessary, especially since most vegetables, before the arrival of the Romans, were used for medicinal rather than culinary purposes.

The cereals, which were usually cut just below the ear, had to be dried in order to improve their keeping properties and to prevent the grain from germinating. Primitive drying kilns were constructed over circular hearths, above which the grain was placed. Quite frequently it became mildly roasted, while some dropped into the edges of the fire, so becoming charred. It is the presence of charred grains that enables archaeologists to say to what use a particular hearth was put. Somewhat naturally, grain which had been over-heated was not fit for seed corn, and it is likely that the latter was dried by more natural means and then stored in large pottery jars or even in small square granaries in which it could be kept insulated from damp and rodents. The grain for consumption was, in many places during the Iron Age, stored in large pits dug in the ground. Providing the pit was kept well sealed, little spoilage occurred, but once a pit was opened, all the contents had to be removed together, for modern experiments have shown that damage would occur if it was resealed. Moreover, storage in pits could only be used where the underlying strata consisted of porous rock or other material; in consequence most are found associated with settlements or farms in the chalk or limestone regions of southern and eastern England. Elsewhere other methods must have been employed, but it is often difficult to identify them.

When required for use the grain was ground into coarse flour or meal on small hand-operated millstones. Although rotary querns were introduced by the La Tène immigrants to Britain, it is likely that the older type of saddle quern continued in use in many places. These were flat, roughly rectangular pieces of suitable rock, sometimes cut so that while the long axis was horizontal to the ground, the short axis dipped to one side, causing the flour to be rubbed out on that side only, thus making its collection easier. Rotary querns, with flattish bottom, and beehive-shaped upper, stones, were fed with the grain through a hopper-like opening in the top. The upper stone, moving round an iron or wooden pivot fixed in the lower, was turned by a wooden handle inserted in a specially cut socket in its side.

The Iron Age agricultural economy probably relied to a great extent on an annual, autumn slaughter of surplus beasts, among which cattle, sheep and pigs would have been the most numerous. Although some hay may have been gathered and dried, it was probably insufficient to maintain anything but the smallest herd throughout the winter. As a result only the basic breeding stock would have been kept, while the remainder would have been killed to provide a good supply of smoked or salted meat as well as leather and skins from the hides. Smoking of meat must have been an extremely simple operation, for it had only to be hung in joints or strips from the roof of the average house to be adequately cured by the smoke which endlessly rose from the fire towards a central vent. It is also easy to understand, in this context, the importance of salt in the economy, for not only could it have been used as an alternative method for preserving the flesh, but also for treating the skins to turn them to leather.

In Britain, the houses of all classes of society in the Iron Age were, almost without exception for many years, considered by archaeologists to be circular in shape, in contrast to continental types which were often round, but also frequently square or rectangular. This apparent difference seemed to emphasise once more the essential insularity of Britain. However, now that far more excavation has taken place in recent years, it can be seen that the assumption was not entirely correct, and good examples of both square and rectangular houses have been located in a number of places such as in the hill-forts at Crickley Hill and Danebury, and in some of the numerous hill-forts on the Welsh border in Herefordshire. They varied much in size, ranging from small square structures, with each corner set by a post, to rectangular buildings up to 20 m long and 6 m wide. Admittedly, the difference between them and the circular structures has not yet been related to function, and it may be that not all were used for domestic purposes, but represent granaries or stores, or even shrines.

Circular structures of considerable size still, however, are the norm in Britain, and future researches may indeed show that they were also commoner in Gaul than has previously been suspected, for the geographer Strabo, writing about the turn of the first centuries BC and AD, records that the people there lived in large, circular houses built of timber. Most such buildings were constructed round a framework of posts set in the ground and usually surrounded by a ditch and low bank. Some were equipped with projecting porches. The infill of the walls was normally made of wattle

41

or wickerwork, liberally coated on both sides with mud to render it more fireproof and also to improve its insulating capacity. The roofs may have been of cut turf laid like tiles or slates on a modern house, or of thatch. A turf roof would have been weighty so that a strong framework was essential and it is clear from the ground plans of such buildings that quite sophisticated carpentry must have been employed. Sometimes, in places where stone abounded, low dry-stone walls were constructed for the outer shell, and on steeply sloping hillsides the houses were constructed on levelled platforms, made by cutting back into the slope and piling the excavated material on the downhill side. This method of construction can be seen on many northern sites such as the hill-fort at Mam Tor in Derbyshire.

In Cornwall, a typical feature of the Iron Age in both the pre-Roman and Roman periods was the farm, or settlement, usually called a round. In them, three or four circular structures are built against the inner face of the enclosure wall, composed of earth or rubble set between dry-stone facing walls. These appear to be the forerunners of the so-called courtyard houses, in which the enclosure wall is thickened on the inner face to absorb the circular structures, leaving a small open courtyard in the middle. Under the latter circumstances, each structure is normally called a 'room' of one house. By arguing backwards, we may then wonder if the original rounds were for single, rather than multiple, family occupancy with each 'house' in fact representing but one 'room' used for a different purpose than the others, instead of being the dwelling of a complete family group. If this was so, it would be possible to argue that enclosures appearing to contain more than one 'house' need not always contain more than one family, with important implications for calculations concerning the size of the population of Britain at the time.

The foregoing remarks apply largely to the pre-Belgic Iron Age in Britain. Consequently, they remain appropriate for those parts of the country untouched by the Belgae where they may, in many places, even be extended to cover the period of the Roman occupation. In the Belgic areas, however, it is surprising that the new immigrants, despite their acknowledged technical superiority in other spheres, had little to add to the methods of constructing houses. Indeed in many instances there even seems to have been a lowering of standards. Admittedly, no building has yet been excavated which could be equated, for instance, with the royal palaces of Verica or Cunobelin. They may, indeed, have occupied better-quality residences, but they remain to be located. For the remainder, house plans seem to follow the traditional British pattern, although one completely excavated example at Canterbury was different. The floor had been sunk some 0.6 m below ground level, very much in the manner of the later, Saxon buildings known as *grübenhäuser*; it was sub-rectangular in shape and the walls, which had been reconstructed more than once, were erected round posts set in the ground. Hearths were constructed of roughly-made slabs of baked clay. Yet it is not impossible that any new building techniques introduced by Belgic migrants could have left little or no trace of their existence for archaeologists to uncover. Some buildings, occasionally attested in the Roman and later periods, were constructed on a framework of beams placed on, or even supported above, the surface, so increasing the life of the timber by reducing its tendency to rot when embedded in the ground, but unfortunately leaving little or no characteristic trace in the soil.

References have already been made, in passing, to the greatly increasing volume of trade which occurred between Britain and the continent in the period between Caesar and Claudius. One of the most popular imports, judging from the number of amphorae, or containers, was wine. These are found on many sites in Hertfordshire and Essex and even further afield, as at the *oppidum* at Bagendon, near Cirencester. Such vessels were, however, also used for transporting other liquids like olive oil and fish sauce, and it is not usually possible to distinguish the original contents, unless, as was sometimes the case, they were indicated by a graffito or a painted legend on the outer surface. Other types of pottery also reached Britain and top-quality tableware manufactured at Arretium in northern Italy travelled via Gaul, which also contributed a wide range of finer wares, like platters and cups. In addition, on the tables of the rich there would have been silver and bronze vessels of Mediterranean manufacture. The geographer Strabo lists

20 Imported Italian amphora of Dressel Type 1 from a La Tène III burial at Welwyn Garden City (Herts.)

21 Imported silver cups of Mediterranean origin from La Tène III burials at (*left*) Welwyn Garden City and (*right*) Welwyn (Herts.)

both exports from, and imports to, Britain. It is an interesting catalogue as it shows what we might expect when trade is carried on between an under-developed country and a more progressive one. The exports from Britain consist almost entirely of basic raw materials and foodstuffs, such as cereals, cattle, gold, silver, iron and hides, together with slaves and dogs. Entering the country, on the other hand, were all manner of manufactured articles and luxury goods.

**22** Miniature bronze shield (66mm long) from Breedon-on-the-Hill hill-fort (Leics.). Such miniature weapons were normally used as votive offerings in Celtic shrines

Cunobelin's kingdom, sitting astride the main trade routes, would no doubt have prospered, while his absorption of the Trinovantian lands may be seen, in part, as a desire to control the trade and gain possession of the coastal ports through which it passed.

Superstition played a major part in every aspect of life of the people of Celtic descent. They imagined their world to be peopled by all manner of spiritual manifestations, mostly of only local importance, but united in that most represented the veneration of abstract powers or natural objects. Most of our knowledge of Celtic religious practices and beliefs comes from the Roman period, by which time they had more frequently taken on a visual or epigraphic form. Consequently, when considering such evidence, we can never be entirely certain that we are dealing with an unsullied Celtic cult, or with one which has received a veneer of classicism. Nevertheless, there survives a small body of evidence, untouched by outside influences, which indicates their religious beliefs. Most natural objects were imbued with some spiritual significance; especially popular were rivers, springs and wells, and they were frequently associated with a concept of fertility. But almost any tree, rock, place, bird or beast could have its resident spirit whose propitiation was of the utmost importance. In many instances, no formal buildings or ceremonies were required. Nevertheless, some deities grew in importance and their presence was then recognised by the erection of a temple or shrine in the vicinity, with attendant priests to carry out the necessary sacrifices or make the offerings which were required. Under such circumstances the power of the deity could receive wider acclaim, so taking on a regional or even national importance, and it is at this level that we come across the official priesthood of the Celts — the Druids.

Unfortunately the Druids have been invested with more romantic myth than almost any other aspect of antiquity.

But they were the dominant priesthood of the Celts, and also exercised considerable political power. In view of the bad press which they received at the hands of classical authors, who recounted their savage rites of human sacrifice, they have probably been given less than their due. There is little doubt of the powerful hold that they maintained over the tribal peoples of north-western Europe, by which they obtained some cohesion between otherwise continuously warring bodies. Something of their strength is indicated by Caesar, who records that any man or tribe that incurred their displeasure was shunned by others for fear of dire misfortunes falling upon them. So the Druids probably saw in the advancing Roman armies a threat which indicated the end of their sway and consequently organised as much resistance as possible. Ultimately outlawed in Gaul, the hard core probably fled to Britain, so perhaps by their fanaticism increasing in the British tribes the will to resist. We might wonder at the part they played in turning the Catuvellauni against the Romans after the death of Cunobelin. It seems likely that their influence, as much as any, lay behind the assembling of a 'British', as opposed to a

23 Sacrificial scene of the late second century BC depicted on the Gundestrup Cauldron, Denmark

purely tribal, army to resist the forces of both Caesar and Claudius. It has even been suggested that Druidic influence lay behind the Boudiccan rebellion of AD 60, since a major revolt in the heart of the province might well have diverted the attention of the Roman army from the capture of their main religious stronghold on the island of Anglesey. When an airfield was being constructed on the island during the last war, a remarkable hoard of metalwork was discovered

**24** Slave-gang chain from the Llyn Cerrig Bach hoard of Iron Age metal work

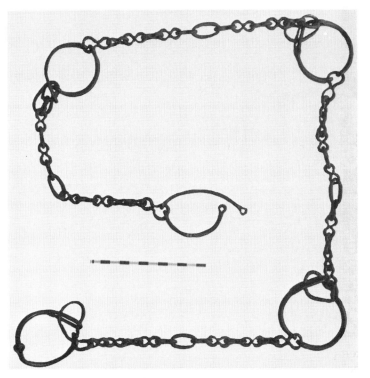

in a bog. It was shown that the objects were derived from many parts of Britain, and that they probably represented gifts or offerings made by different tribal peoples, so demonstrating the wide influence of the main Druidic sanctuary; the pieces had probably been cast into a lake or spring of great sanctity, in order to propitiate some water deity. Among the more evocative objects was a gang chain for a group of five slaves or prisoners. It is not difficult to imagine the fate of those who were once shackled by it. That Druids officiated over the mainstream of Celtic religion is further indicated by Tacitus' description of the Roman assault on the island. Apart from venerating water, as clearly indicated by the metalwork thrown into the bog, Tacitus mentions that, after the assault, the Romans cut down the sacred groves of trees, which obviously had some major significance. Moreover a considerable knowledge of astronomy and philosophy was attributed to the Druids, and they were able to compute calendrical cycles involving both the sun and moon. Their position as national leaders was therefore assured.

Clearly then in Celtic religion, the central feature was the sanctified object, be it animal, tree, rock or spring. There is, however, some evidence for the existence of subsidiary

temples and shrines, the basic pattern of building usually being indicated by the plan of the supposed Iron Age temple excavated at Heathrow; it appears to be a central, almost square structure surrounded on all sides by a portico. As such, it closely resembles the type of temple well-attested later in parts of Britain and Gaul which are known collectively as Romano-Celtic temples. Fortunately, the existence of a temple on a site during the Roman period can sometimes be taken to indicate the sanctity of a preceding Iron Age building. For instance at both Frilford (Berks.) and Thistleton Dyer (Leics.) masonry buildings of the Roman period overlie circular timber structures belonging to the Iron Age. Without the presence of the later temples over them, both would probably have been interpreted as domestic dwellings; so the difficulties of interpretation can be demonstrated. Recently, also, suggestions have been made that the square, four-posted houses mentioned earlier

25 Basilican Romano-British temple at Thistleton Dyer (Rutland) built on the site of an earlier, Iron Age circular temple

47

– and the people

in this chapter may have been small domestic shrines.

Burial rites may be considered to be an extension of religious beliefs. The Celts believed in a material existence in an after-life, as they were taught to do so by the Druids, and consequently catered for it in the graves in which they were buried. They also believed that the spirits of the departed could take over the body of the living unless propitiated. So all burials reflected the desires of the deceased to be as well

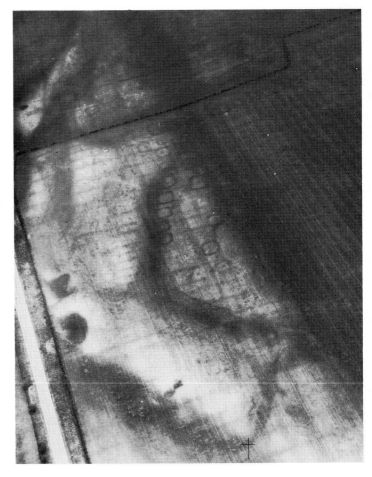

**26** Aerial photograph of a late Iron Age cemetery of square barrows at Burton Fleming (East Yorkshire)

equipped in the after-life as they had been in the present. Weapons, food and drink, buckets, cauldrons, games, ornaments and trinkets were all included in the richer graves, while the poor had to make do with lesser objects. Some large cemeteries of the later La Tène period have been located in Kent, Essex and Hertfordshire, notably at Aylesford, Swarling, Welwyn and Verulamium. Richly furnished in many cases, they were sometimes enclosed within a square, marked by a ditch. Other equally important burials of a slightly different character have been discovered in parts of Yorkshire, where individual graves sometimes included complete carts or chariots. Mostly, such interments would have been of chieftains or of the warrior class of society, and in almost every case the body was cremated.

The material obtained by the excavation of these burials, although including many pieces of imported pottery, glass or metalwork, also provides a large mass of home-produced goods that illustrate the technical proficiency of the craftsmen of the period. In the beginning of the Iron Age, most pottery was probably made by a household as part of normal domestic duties, although there is very early on evidence for the existence of specialist bronzesmiths and blacksmiths. By the later La Tène period, however, it is normal to assume that full-time professional potters were practising their art which included a knowledge of wheel-turned vessels and a greater ability to fire them more evenly. It is strange though that no pottery kiln has yet been found which can be attributed to this period, and, in consequence, it has been suggested that the firing was carried out in clamps. Now, however, we know that during the Roman period kilns were erected above ground level and that, by modern experiment, they worked satisfactorily; so it may be assumed that similar kilns were used in the immediate pre-Roman Iron Age. Such kilns can leave little trace of their existence, often no more than a circular burnt patch on the ground which can easily be taken, in the absence of critical evidence, for a normal hearth.

Most other crafts can be identified in later Iron Age Britain, ranging from the professional smiths, and perhaps carpenters, to the manufacturers, mostly on a domestic scale, of cloth and basket-work. Boat-builders certainly knew their job and were capable of constructing quite large, sea-worthy vessels.

It is, however, the work of the bronzesmith and blacksmith which demonstrate perhaps more than any other crafts, the technical skill available, both in design and execution. The iron fire-dogs found in a number of burials would not disgrace a modern hearth, while the complicated, often asymmetrical, designs with their curvilinear ornament and restrained enamelling, to be seen on articles of war, such as the Battersea or Witham shields, must represent a peak of achievement, both artistically and technically, of more than competent bronzesmiths probably working for rich patrons. Admittedly that peak had been passed by the time of the Roman invasion in AD 43, but the tradition was still strong enough to survive in the north and west, and so to

– and the people

27 Celtic art. Detail of a bronze flagon handle of the fourth century BC from Basse-Yutz, Thionville-Est, Moselle

**28** Celtic art. Detail of the circular bronze shield boss found in the river Thames at Wandsworth

some extent maintained, with only minor modification, an artistic link between pre- and post-Roman Britain that surfaced from time to time in the Roman period with objects like the Aesica brooch from Greatchesters on Hadrian's wall.

# Roman successes — and failures

The year AD 43 brought both failure and success for Roman policy towards Britain. The failure came first. In the changed circumstances, it was no longer possible to keep up the diplomatic contacts with the British tribes which had been begun by Augustus and maintained by Tiberius. Even before the principate of Claudius, the abortive attempt at invasion by the emperor Gaius Caligula indicated that established Roman policy towards Britain lay in ruins. With the uncompromisingly anti-Roman attitude displayed by Caratacus and Togodumnus, following the expulsion of Verica from his southern kingdom, the time had come for military force to replace diplomacy. Some, in Rome, saw this at last as the completion of a job long delayed since Caesar's day.

It is likely that the expulsion of Verica proved to be the event which tipped the scales in favour of Roman military intervention. Before, when Tincommius had been expelled, it had been possible for Augustus to continue his alliance with the new Atrebatic ruler, for no break had occurred in the dynastic succession. Now, however, Claudius was faced with a professedly anti-Roman usurper in their territory, who controlled much of the British south coast, and who would not, apparently, negotiate. In modern terms, diplomatic relations were broken off, an action made more necessary after the request had been made for Verica's extradition.

But other factors also influenced the Roman decision to invade Britain. There was Claudius' personal desire for military success; legendary stories of Britain's mineral wealth had been circulating for some time in Rome; Britain remained the last refuge of the Druids, whose extermination was deemed desirable for political as well as religious reasons; there was Caesar's 'unfinished' business in Britain. But above all, there was the wrong to a Roman ally, a client king, to be avenged, which, in so doing, would also accomplish the permanent defeat of a long-standing enemy, the Catuvellauni. At that time, Rome relied heavily on alliances with native princes near or beyond the frontiers to maintain peace, so ensuring a considerable economy of Roman man-

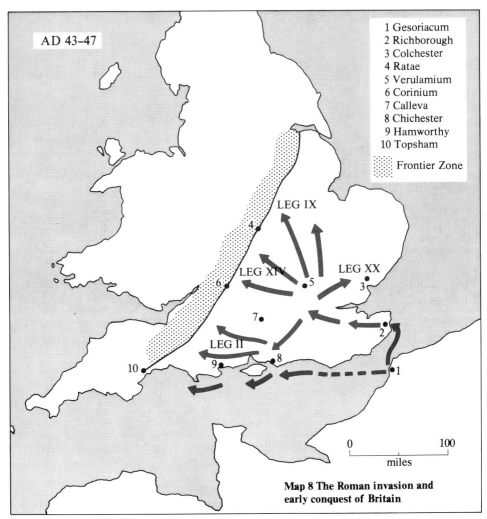

AD 43-47

1 Gesoriacum
2 Richborough
3 Colchester
4 Ratae
5 Verulamium
6 Corinium
7 Calleva
8 Chichester
9 Hamworthy
10 Topsham

Frontier Zone

LEG IX

LEG XIV

LEG XX

LEG II

Map 8 The Roman invasion and
early conquest of Britain

power. To have allowed Verica's expulsion to pass without
vigorous action to reinstate him would have called in
question, therefore, a whole sphere of imperial policy, and
would have made other client rulers reassess the value of
their alliances.

In addition, there was a question of military strategy to be
considered. It had for some time been realised in Rome that
too large a provincial garrison, commanded by an un-
scrupulous governor, could be a threat to the emperor's
position. Consequently since Augustus' principate it had
been the practice to distribute the legions evenly throughout
all the frontier provinces, so that theoretically no one
governor had excess strength. The situation now required a
military force to be deployed against Britain, either to protect the coast of north Gaul, or to occupy the country. But

already the army on the Rhine was one legion over strength and to have added yet more troops on the Channel coast would have been in direct contradiction to established policy. Moreover, an additional garrison in Gaul would have caused far-reaching logistical problems. The solution lay in the occupation of Britain, which would place the garrison in safety across the sea, while newly-conquered territory would provide the food and other materials needed

to maintain it. The invasion was accomplished by four legions, commanded by Aulus Plautius, and detached from the Rhine and Danube frontiers: Legio II Augusta, Legio IX Hispana, Legio XIV Gemina and Legio XX Valeria, together with auxiliary cavalry and infantry. Some uncertainty still exists in the minds of archaeologists as to the places at which this army landed in Britain, although we know that it sailed from Boulogne. The only place to provide indisputable evidence for its arrival is Richborough in east Kent, where a fortified beach-head was first constructed, to be rapidly replaced by a stores depot of considerable size. Attempts have been made to argue that landings also took place on the south coast, in particular in the neighbourhood of Chichester, in order to reinstate Verica and expel the Catuvellaunian usurpers. Although there is no specific evidence for such a landing, it would have made sound strategic sense, even if, tactically, it might have been questioned. The invasion was an overwhelming success, despite some hard fighting and some difficult moments, and within a matter of months, Claudius himself led his victorious army into the British capital at Camulodunum, from where battle groups fanned outwards and rapidly took control of most of lowland Britain, so achieving the primary objectives of defeating, and occupying the territory of, the Catuvellauni and reinstating Verica in his kingdom.

**29** Richborough, Kent: the landing place of the Roman army in AD 43. The original shore line is indicated by the tree-covered scarp to the top left of the photo. The walls of the later Saxon Shore fort are just visible in the trees in front of the power-station cooling towers

53

## Roman successes – and failures

**30** (a) Fragmentary dedication (*CIL* VI, 920) from the triumphal arch of Claudius, erected in Rome in AD 52, recording his British victories, and (b) restored version with three other fragments. The whole inscription would have read:

*Ti(berio) Clau[dio Drusi f(ilio) Cai]sari Augu[sto Germani]co Pontific[i Maxim(o) Trib(unicia) Potes]tat(e) XI Co(n)s(uli) V Im[p(eratori) XXII Cens(ori) Patri Pa]triae Senatus Po[pulusque] Ro[manus Q]uod Reges Brit[anniorum] XI D[evictos sine] ulla iactu[ra in deditionem acceperit] gentesque b[arbaras trans oceanum] primus indici[onem populi Romani redegerit*

'To the emperor Tiberius Claudius, son of Drusus, Caesar Augustus Germanicus, Pontifex Maximus, with tribunician power for the eleventh time, Consul for the fifth time, saluted as Imperator twenty-two (?) times, Censor, Father of his country. (Erected by) the Senate and People of Rome because he received the formal submission of eleven British kings, overcome without loss, and because he was the first to bring barbarian tribesmen across the Ocean under the sway of the Roman people.'

Opinion is divided as to whether it was, from the very beginning, the Roman intention to occupy the whole of Britain, or whether the reaching of the primary objectives, as outlined above, was the only goal, from which imperial policy had slowly to depart as it was realised that no permanent solution to the British problem had been achieved. Whatever their intentions, the earliest frontier defences were laid out along a line drawn from Devon to north Lincolnshire, and enshrined the road which we know today as the Fosse Way; it rapidly proved untenable. While it may have been tactically successful in regulating movement into and out of the new province, strategically it allowed too great a freedom for the hostile tribes of Wales, now strengthened by the presence of Caratacus, who had escaped capture in the earlier battles; they could unite at will and attack where they wished. At first, this new threat was met by moving garrisons up to and slightly beyond the valley of the river Severn, which for a time countered the enemy's efforts, although some firm action was on more than one occasion called for in south Wales.

Predominantly, therefore, in the late 40s and 50s the main danger to the Roman dispositions lay in Wales, since the northern frontier, embracing the line of the rivers Trent and Humber, was controlled by a friendly ally, Queen Cartimandua and her Brigantian tribe. It might also be argued at this point that, had it been the Roman intention to conquer the whole of Britain, they would have resumed the advance into Wales sooner and with much more energy than they did. Ample time had already been granted to consolidate the army's position. Compulsory requisitions of food and supplies from the native peoples — the *annona* — could have been fully organised within a few years of its arrival, so that logistics presented no difficulty. As it was, the three governors who succeeded Aulus Plautius contented themselves with holding operations or with comparatively minor campaigns in south Wales as and when the opportunity arose, or occasion demanded. It is likely that some of the marching camps which have been identified in the area should rightly be attributed to their actions. Not all the actions were successful and twice the Roman army was humiliated by defeat; the balance was, however, corrected by the capture of Caratacus, who, after losing a major battle in central Wales, had been forced to flee to Cartimandua in the north and was promptly handed over to Rome.

The appointment of Suetonius Paullinus as governor in the late 50s seems to have marked a change in policy towards Britain, which perhaps began to foresee the conquest of Wales as a necessity for peace. Paullinus attacked in north Wales, probably after defeating the Silures in the south, and aimed for the heart of Druidic power, the island of Anglesey. All was going well when he received information of a serious revolt in the south-east.

The Boudiccan rebellion of AD 60 was compounded of many contributory factors. Over-zealousness, arrogance and greed were displayed by both sides, while the Romans displayed their usual ready ability to trample the susceptible feelings of the natives.

The consolidation of the earliest frontier line from the Severn to the Trent in the late 40s had brought about the removal of most of the garrisons from south-east England. The military government, which their presence represented, was replaced by civilian, local administrations of three different types. In the van was the newly-founded settlement of retired legionaries near the site of Cunobelin's capital at Colchester. Given the title of a *colonia*, it required a considerable tract of land for the grants made to its new inhabitants, each legionary receiving a plot both within and outside the town. The land was probably acquired by direct requisition, leading to much antagonism on the part of the Trinovantes, who, very likely, also lost the site of their principal religious centre at Gosbecks nearby. Admittedly it would seem that they were compensated by the provision of a brand new site for a tribal capital at Chelmsford, although subsequent developments tend to show that this was not acceptable, and that the major grudge which they consequently bore the Romans continued to rankle. Also included among the new civilian authorities were two client kingdoms. Verica's original state was maintained in the south, but now under the rule of his successor, Cogidubnus. In East Anglia, the tribe of the Iceni was likewise constituted, although they seem to have been less prepared to settle down under the new regime; a minor revolt had to be put down amongst them in AD 49. In parallel with the client kingdoms were the native civilian authorities constituted as *civitates*, of which there were probably no more than three in the early period.

In addition to the long standing grievance of the Trinovantes, further trouble arose when the Icenian kingdom was reduced to the normal status of a *civitas* following the death of its ruler, Prasutagus, in AD 59 or 60. The attempts at reduction were forcibly resisted by his widow, Boudicca, and her followers. The governor and most of the army was in north Wales and there seemed little to stop the Iceni, who were rapidly joined by the Trinovantes, from securing their freedom. The new towns at Colchester, London and Verulamium were sacked before Paullinus could take any action, but, ultimately he was able to bring the rebels to battle in the Midlands and defeat them.

The rebellion, despite Paullinus' final success, was undoubtedly a disaster for Roman policy towards Britain. Yet it may be that it was the executants who were more at fault than the policy itself. Equally it was a disaster for the Iceni,

**31** Pottery from a shop at Colchester burnt in the Boudiccan rebellion

who never seem to have recovered fully from its effects, and who remained thereafter a somewhat backward and penurious tribe. The Trinovantes perhaps fared a little better; at any rate they appear to have regained control of their religious centre outside Colchester.

In so far as Roman policy was concerned, the province remained at a near standstill for almost a whole decade, while repair of the physical damage seems, in some places such as Verulamium, to have taken even longer. Indeed the worst consequence of the rebellion may be seen as the inducement of a crisis of confidence in the pro-Roman members of the British community, who would normally

have been relied upon to uphold law and order and implement, at native level, the whole process which we may call
romanisation. The failure of Roman arms to protect their
lives and property, therefore, had far-reaching effects.

But the turn of the wheel of fortune in a completely different direction less than a decade after the rebellion gave
rise to circumstances from which Britain was ultimately to
benefit. The civil war which began in the empire after Nero's
suicide in AD 68 finally threw up the emperor Vespasian
and saw the end of the supremacy of the Julio-Claudian
dynasty. Vespasian already knew Britain, having commanded a legion in the invasion army, and his accession saw
a much firmer policy being adopted towards the province.
The period of drift which had followed the first push of the
40s, and which was not always favourable to the Romans,
was now replaced by a strategy which possibly, at first,
anticipated the conquest of the whole of Britain as
its ultimate aim. First came the defeat of the Brigantes,
who by now had risen against their pro-Roman queen,
Cartimandua, causing her to seek refuge with her allies. A
masterly campaign conducted by Petillius Cerealis so routed
them that, when nearly a decade later their territory was
occupied, little or no opposition seems to have been en-
countered. Next came the settlement of the Welsh problem
with a firm grasp being taken by Julius Frontinus, who
instituted a system of garrison forts in the hostile territories.
Finally, Julius Agricola occupied the Brigantian territory and
within six years had not only defeated the Caledonians in an
extended series of campaigns, but had also advanced the
Roman province to the edge of the Scottish highlands. The
period of AD 70–86 was one of unqualified success, but
then the impetus was lost. What factor was responsible for
the halt being called, we do not know. We may suspect,
however, that it was the increasing drain that Britain represented in terms of manpower to the empire, manpower that
was becoming increasingly needed elsewhere. Occupation
as far as the Highlands was one thing; occupation of the
Highlands, with their difficult terrain, would have been
altogether another problem and would have required a large
sedentary garrison. Moreover, it was probably appreciated
by then that little would be gained by taking over the whole
area.

Soon after Agricola's recall, the need arose to reduce the
British garrison in order to provide troops for service on the
Danube frontier, and it proved impossible to maintain even
the Agricolan dispositions in the face of these demands. A
whole legion, probably accompanied by some auxiliaries,

was withdrawn from Britain, which made necessary considerable retrenchment of the surviving forces. Strategy required that the new legionary fortresses at York, Chester and Caerleon should be occupied, so the legion based in Scotland at Inchtuthil was withdrawn, perhaps first to Wroxeter and then to Chester. With it came those auxiliary units stationed alongside it on the Highland fringe. Indeed no fort beyond the Forth-Clyde isthmus seems to have been

occupied after this reorganisation and it is likely that this narrow neck of land was intended to be the new frontier. South of the line, however, many forts were entirely rebuilt, often to a stronger and larger pattern, as if to emphasise the need to retain a firm hold on southern Scotland. Central in this new scheme was the fort at Newstead, apparently occupied by a battle group composed of legionaries and auxiliary cavalry, a rare arrangement more reminiscent of the conquest period, and indicative of the importance attached to this Lowland site. In many ways this reappraisal of the northern frontier of Britain made better strategic sense than the scheme imposed by Agricola, but it had one chief weakness. It was too detached from the northern Caledonians, who could combine at will in the plains around Perth and

32 Aerial photograph of the legionary fortress at Inchtuthil (Perthshire), from the south-east

attack where they chose. It therefore suffered the same defect as the first frontier to be placed against Wales.

The new arrangements lasted until the early second century, when it would appear that disaster struck the outlying forts in the Lowlands, and many were burnt to the ground, but whether by enemy action or by deliberate evacuation cannot be decided. The withdrawal from southern Scotland may have been caused by the need for more troops for Trajan's Dacian campaigns. Perhaps, as one authority considers, the local population capitalised on a moment of confusion caused by the evacuation, and attacked certain forts. Be that as it may, a new frontier was established along the road, the Stanegate, built by Agricola to run from Corbridge to Carlisle. Here were placed extra forts in addition to the two already in being at the terminal points, and it is possible that two detached signal towers on the line of the later Hadrianic frontier also belonged to this system. Moreover, and as if to indicate that the phase of unlimited expansion had for the time finished in Britain, the three legionary fortresses at York, Caerleon and Chester were entirely rebuilt, masonry now taking the place of timber construction. Similar improvements were also carried out in some auxiliary forts in Wales and the north.

The dispositions made early in Trajan's principate held until the end of his reign, when there was another serious uprising in the north, which may have involved not only the tribes of Lowland Scotland but also the Brigantes.

It had now been demonstrated often enough in the empire, not only in Britain but also in other provinces, that frontier systems which incorporated a single chain or zone of forts, albeit in conjunction with a natural barrier such as a river, were inadequate to cope with a full-scale war or rebellion. Isolated attempts had already been made on other frontiers to couple the forts to a continuous barrier of a palisade or earthen bank. Accordingly, when Hadrian reached Britain on his extended tour of the provinces, it was decreed that the northern frontier should be completely reorganised to include a physical barrier of considerable size, set just north of the Stanegate. So was constructed the work which we know today as Hadrian's Wall.

The Wall itself was but part of an elaborate defensive system which incorporated a series of forts, milecastles, turrets, a great external ditch and a service road set within a controlled area marked by an earthwork, the Vallum. Several major alterations were made to the original plan while construction was still under way, and the resulting appearance of the frontier varied considerably from one end to the other, since the whole of the barrier from the river Irthing to Carlisle was, for speed, built of stacked turf instead of masonry. Nevertheless, in that section, the turrets were of masonry, although the milecastles were constructed of turf and timber. West of Bowness, a series of milecastles and, later, also towers extended down the Cumberland coast and appear to have been associated with a palisade and double-ditched road.

33 Aerial photograph of Hadrian's Wall at Cawfields. The wall follows the line of the scarp and the Cawfields milecastle can be seen near the top edge of the modern quarry. The vallum, with the later crossings cut through it, runs to the rear in a straight line; small temporary camps can be seen to its right

Many arguments and discussions have taken place as to the precise purpose which the Wall was intended to serve. One school of thought maintains that it was never meant to serve as a military fortification or a defensive barrier, and that it was but a masonry equivalent of the wooden palisade on the German frontier, by which passage of people through it could be controlled; as such, it has been reasoned, it would have been little more use than a police post, while the main garrisons in the forts were intended to fight, not on

61

the frontier, but in the outfield beyond. Also cited in support is the occasional bad positioning of the Wall for defence, with higher ground overlooking it to the north. Yet it is hard to reconcile these views with the massive strength of the work. If the barrier was only intended to control the native population, why was a palisade not built, as on the German frontier, especially when, as happened at the western end, speed of completion became a necessity? While it is possible to argue, as some have done, that the original concept of a masonry wall was intended as a grandiose and lasting memorial to Rome's most northerly frontier, it is not so easy to apply such reasoning to a turf wall, and even less so to the palisade which extended westwards from Bowness down the Cumberland coast.

Even if we admit that the large number of mounted troops, in garrison on the frontier, were not there for the purpose of static defence, but were meant to reach out towards an advancing enemy, it is still possible to accept a greater role for the Wall itself beyond that of providing a convenient regulating point for police purposes. In the first place, it must be remembered that on both sides of the northern British frontier the people were an unruly lot who had repeatedly caused trouble to the Roman army, whereas the tribes facing the German frontier were, at the time, more peacefully disposed. This one factor could be sufficient to account for the greatly increased strength of the British frontier. On the other hand, to describe it as an impregnable defensive system is perhaps to overstate the case in the other direction. The impregnability of any physical barrier, no matter how large, can only be calculated in terms of the quality and quantity of its defenders. Remove those defenders and, sooner or later, the attackers will find a way round, under or over any barrier. Consequently, as a last resort, the garrisons, even if they were normally expected to fight beyond it, could have manned the Wall and used it in its defensive capacity in a way that would hardly have been feasible on the German frontier.

The question of the tactics employed by the fighting garrison also raises an important issue with regard to the purpose of Hadrian's Wall. If mobile troops are to function properly it is necessary for them to have absolutely secure bases from which to operate, otherwise their efficiency would rapidly decline. The Wall provided those bases and enabled them to be protected from attack when the garrisons were performing their rightful duties elsewhere.

We may conclude, therefore, that Hadrian's Wall fulfilled a combination of uses. It acted as a control point for the peaceful movement of peoples; it provided secure bases for its garrisons, from which they could operate with maximum effect on either side of the frontier, and, as a last resort, it possessed a defensive capacity which could be employed should the occasion arise.

The construction work on the Wall continued for over a decade, and, even then, we still cannot be entirely certain when the turf wall was replaced by masonry. It may not have happened until the retreat from Scotland took place several decades later, when Hadrian's Wall once more became the northern frontier. It is worth noting, however, that most native hostility appears to have been directed against its western end. That was the sector that had to be completed in a hurry with turfwork; there was placed, at Stanwix, just outside Carlisle, the senior officer of the whole garrison, who commanded the only milliary regiment of cavalry in Britain. Such regiments were normally placed where need for both strength and mobility were greatest. At the west end, also, were built three outpost forts to guard the approaches to the frontier.

The effectiveness of Hadrian's Wall is usually summed up as being a tactical success but a strategic failure. Yet hindsight enables us to view it as the most successful frontier work in Britain, to which return was made when all other possibilities had been exhausted. It had weaknesses, but it should be recorded that it was apparently only once completely over-run when the garrison was in residence and, on that occasion, treachery was the cause of its fall.

But despite the effectiveness of the Wall, two further attempts were to be tried to establish a more northerly frontier, before return to it was finally made. In AD 140, following the accession of Antoninus Pius as emperor, a major reconsideration of Britain's northern frontier was again put in hand. In consequence, an extensive campaign was launched into Scotland with the final outcome being the construction, between the Forth and the Clyde, of a new frontier work usually called the Antonine Wall.

There were many differences between this and Hadrian's Wall, chiefly in the materials of construction and in the disposition of the garrisons. The linear barrier was built throughout its length of cut and stacked turf laid on a cobbled foundation; beyond it was a large ditch. There was apparently no regular system of milecastles or turrets; neither was there an earthwork to the rear of the installations as on Hadrian's Wall. Nevertheless, the most recent views have suggested that not all the installations were contemporary, but that, as with Hadrian's Wall, alterations were introduced into the plan before building was complete. Possibly only six forts of the known or implied nineteen were original and these may have been at first supported by intervening fortlets, which in some cases were only later replaced by larger forts. Ultimately the garrisons were contained in these forts, normally but not always attached to the barrier, of many different sizes and placed much closer together than on the more southerly frontier line. Moreover,

**34** Aerial photograph of the Antonine Wall at Rough Castle. To the right of the main ditch can be seen a group of *liliae* in a clearing among the trees

not all internal buildings were built of masonry, as return was made in many instances to timber structures. Indeed, we might be excused for viewing the whole frontier as something of a cautious experiment, which, if it did not succeed, could be readily abandoned without too much lost effort. If, on the other hand, it proved successful, the construction could be made more permanent by replacing the turfwork and timber with masonry. These changes were almost certainly introduced from lessons learnt on Hadrian's Wall. In one respect, however, there was a

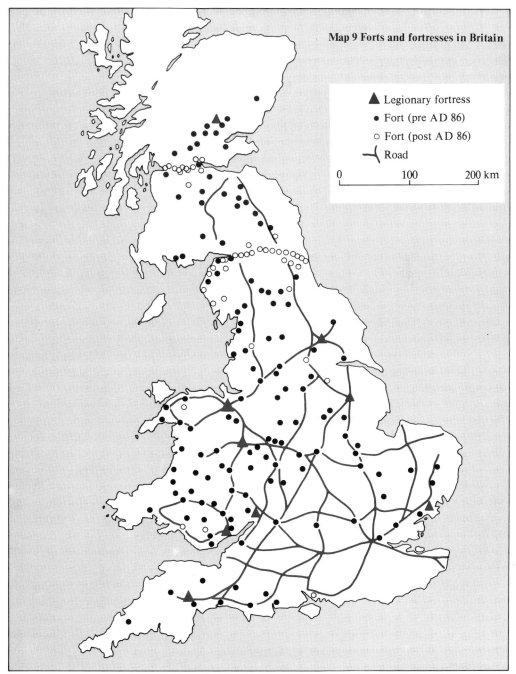

Map 9 Forts and fortresses in Britain

▲ Legionary fortress
• Fort (pre AD 86)
○ Fort (post AD 86)
Road

0    100    200 km

similarity. Outpost forts stretched as far north as Strageath and possibly Bertha, presumably duplicating the function of those that had protected the approaches to the west end of Hadrian's Wall.

With the new frontier established in Scotland, close to a line that Agricola had once used some sixty years earlier, Hadrian's Wall was now freely opened to allow passage in both directions. Gates were removed from the milecastles and the Vallum to the rear had many extra crossings made. Only in the forts is there some evidence of small legionary detachments caring for the fabric, and this to some extent supports the view that the new frontier was perhaps an experimental work and that, when it was constructed, it was not known if return would have to be made to the earlier line. But for some fourteen years the new fortifications held successfully.

The construction of permanent physical barriers as a northern frontier had repercussions elsewhere. The concentration of troops which they required for effective manning could only be obtained by the evacuation of other forts further south. So under Hadrian we find extensive areas of south Wales and also east of the Pennines released from military control, while, under Antoninus Pius, further relaxation occurred in Wales. The latter was necessitated by the need to place garrisons once more in southern Scotland in addition to those planted on and beyond the frontier. It is probably true to say that the army in Britain was now stretched to its maximum and that hostile action in the ungarrisoned parts could only be met quickly by the withdrawal of troops from the frontier.

When hostile action came it was from within the province and not from beyond the borders. In AD 154, there appears to have been a serious rebellion in Brigantia, which caused the immediate evacuation of the Antonine Wall and the forts on either side of it, coupled with the demolition of the installations. With by far the largest concentration of auxiliary troops placed in Scotland, the brunt of the early fighting must have been borne by the more southerly-based legions at York, Chester and Caerleon. There were probably casualties, for, when a new governor arrived to settle the rebellion, he brought with him reinforcements for all three legions from the German provinces, although it is not impossible that the legions had been under strength, with detachments serving elsewhere in the empire. Some forts seem to have been successfully attacked by the rebels and at least two were burnt to the ground.

After the rebellion had been suppressed, there followed a

reassessment of the position, brought about by the shortage of troops. Scotland remained unoccupied for the time being, while Hadrian's Wall was hurriedly restored to active commission. Moreover, work was started on rebuilding forts in Brigantia, as far as its southern border, with a view to increasing again the number of military garrisons in the territory, and presumably, by so doing, returning large areas to military government. The rebellion, therefore, marks a

Roman successes – and failures

**35** Antonine inscription (*RIB* 1322) from the river Tyne at Newcastle. It reads:

*Imp(eratore) Antonino Aug(usto) Pio p(atri) pat(riae) vexil(l)atio leg(ioni) II Aug(ustae) et leg(ioni) VI Vic(trici) et leg(ioni) XX V(aleriae) V(ictrici) con(t)r(i)buti ex Ger(maniis) duobus sub Iulio Vero leg(ato) Aug(usti) pro p(raetore)*

'(Set up) for the Emperor Antonius Augustus Pius, father of his Country, (by) the detachment contributed from the two Germanies for the Second Legion Augusta and the Sixth Legion Victrix and the Twentieth Legion Valeria Victrix, under Julius Verus, emperor's propraetorian legate.'

The inscription refers to reinforcements being brought to Britain from Germany *c.* AD 155, probably as the result of a Brigantian rebellion

failure of a more enlightened piece of Roman policy. The calculated gamble taken first by Hadrian and followed by Antoninus Pius, to give a large section of the Brigantes the opportunity to run their own local administration, had not worked. The people were clearly not yet ready to accept peaceful romanisation, with all that it meant, and preferred to retain their continuing hostile attitude to Rome. Accordingly the Roman coat had to be cut to suit the British cloth, with its inevitable consequences for the northern frontier. But the policy was not abandoned by the government without further effort at its implementation. Once more, perhaps in AD 159, the army advanced to Scotland and re-established its presence on the Antonine Wall and once more Hadrian's Wall appears to have been deprived of its garrisons. But not for long, and an increasingly threatening situation required a new governor to withdraw again after probably no more than a year or so.

The reoccupation of Hadrian's Wall as the northern frontier was accompanied on this occasion by the provision of more outpost forts, on the main road, Dere Street, leading northwards from Corbridge; they appear to represent,

when taken in conjunction with the three already in existence, a more rigid containment of the hostile tribes of south-
west Scotland, the Selgovae and Novantae. Indeed, the
extra fortifications along the road seem deliberately
designed to protect the Votadini, a friendly tribe to the east,
from attack by their neighbours. Although the frontier now
remained stable, the remainder of the second century
passed in a state of near-continuous turbulence. On at least
one occasion considerable reinforcements had to be brought
to Britain, presumably just to maintain the existing dispositions. On another, slightly later, it seems that the Wall was
itself penetrated by an enemy attack, but probably on a
limited front. It is not impossible that the late second-
century destruction of the fort at Corbridge took place then,
although it is far more likely to have been in a later war. But
these serious, albeit comparatively minor, episodes pale
before the disaster which overtook not only Britain but also
the empire in the last decade of the century.

At the very end of AD 192 the emperor Commodus, who
was not one of the most commendable members of the
imperial household, was assassinated. There followed one
of the costly civil wars for the succession which were to
become increasingly common in the third century and
which had already been anticipated on the death of Nero,
over a hundred years before. On this occasion four con-
testants made their claims, one of whom was Clodius
Albinus, governor of Britain. Two were quickly eliminated
from the struggle leaving Albinus to face Septimius Severus
alone. Albinus gathered together an army from the British
garrisons, crossed the Channel and, being joined by a legion
from Spain, marched south-eastwards across Gaul. He met
Severus near Lyons and was defeated.

In the meantime, Britain, deprived of all but the most
meagre of defences, lay wide open to attack. A confederacy
of tribes from Scotland, together with the Brigantes and
possibly also some of the tribes in north Wales, seized the
opportunity to wreck such empty forts as lay in their path,
including perhaps the legionary fortress at York. Fortunately, however, Albinus had probably had the foresight to
order fortifications to be erected around many towns and
villages in the lowland area, which kept them immune from
assault. The many villages associated with the northern forts
were not so lucky. Undefended, and with their inhabitants
long forbidden by Roman law to carry arms, they had lost
the ability to protect themselves and so suffered in the same
way as their parent forts. Such were the immediate consequences to Britain of a fatal flaw in the Roman constitution,

which did not automatically recognise an heir to a reigning emperor. Others were to follow.

Severus dispatched a succession of governors to Britain who were given the task of ejecting the invaders, suppressing the internal rebels and rebuilding the destroyed installations. It was no easy task since the Scottish confederacy kept up the war and there was some hint that they might be joined by the Caledonian tribes from further north; moreover the Brigantes continued active. Gradually, however, fort by fort, the destruction was rectified. Hadrian's Wall, where it had been damaged, was rebuilt, but not before the hostile forces had been bought off by payment of a large sum. This in itself is indicative of the Roman failure to control the situation by force of arms, most likely brought about by inadequate manpower, and possibly also by vacillation over the decision whether or not to reoccupy southern Scotland. Ultimately Severus himself, acting on the advice of his governor, seized the opportunity of mounting a punitive expedition in Britain and, in AD 208 arrived together with his two sons and considerable reinforcements. But the campaigns that followed then and in the two succeeding years were unable to bring about a decisive conclusion, despite isolated victories; a stalemate could have ensued. The situation changed though when Severus died in York in AD 211, leaving his elder son, Caracalla, to continue the war. This he did not do, but seems instead to have made a satisfactory settlement with the enemy. We know nothing of the terms of the agreement, but they were obviously the most successful that had ever been tried on the northern frontier, for they brought the longest period of apparently uninterrupted peace in that troubled area and moreover, for the first time also, quelled the Brigantes. We can only assume, therefore, that the terms were satisfactory to both sides. Although the northern frontier, now irrevocably placed on Hadrian's Wall, had to be maintained, the cessation of almost constant fighting should have brought with it considerable economies for Rome. For many of the natives in northern England and beyond the frontier, the period of peace brought with it a new prosperity which was reflected in the many villages now rebuilt outside forts, and in the increasing number of farmsteads in the areas. Although still basically of Iron Age character they benefited from having regular markets and access to new technologies and materials. Diplomacy had, on this occasion proved more successful than force. Nevertheless, the diplomatic initiative which had been gained was wisely supported by a strong protective force on the frontier, which, now that the threat

69

of attack from the rear had largely been neutralised, became a military base for a zone of operations stretching far out beyond it. In this zone were the five outpost forts, mostly manned by milliary cohorts containing both infantry and cavalry and supported by more irregular units of scouts, who could range even further afield.

The immediate consequence of the war was, as we have seen, the destruction of forts and villages in the north and in parts of Wales. But for the rest of the province the sequel was probably more deeply felt. It is known that in Spain, where a solitary legion, and presumably many civilians, had supported the cause of Albinus, large-scale confiscation of estates by Severus took place after the struggle. There is no reason to believe that he treated those landowners in Britain who had supported Albinus any more leniently; there must have been many who did so in the hope of reward or preferment in the event of the latter's success. Consequently this civil war could have had far-reaching effects on the British economy, which are, as yet, perhaps not fully recognised or appreciated. It might well be this factor, rather than any other, which caused marked fluctuations in the fortunes of villas in Britain during the third century. If farms had been sequestrated they would presumably either have been retained as imperial estates, or they may have been given or sold to the supporters of Severus. In such circumstances the house, at the centre of a property, may have become superfluous for an owner who already possessed a residence elsewhere, and so be allowed to fall into disrepair. Houses in towns could have suffered similarly, and at Leicester a luxurious dwelling of some important person, immediately north of the forum, was at this time first converted into a factory, before being demolished and its place taken by a large public building. This could represent the donation or sale of confiscated land to the municipal authority.

But although comparative peace had now descended on the northern frontier and on Wales after over a century of almost continuous strife, Britain was not to remain long free from external attack. It would seem that early in the third century, if not before, piratical raiders from northern Europe were becoming bolder in their operations. The North Sea can never have been entirely free of their presence, but now they appear to have turned their attentions to coastal raiding. The fleet which guarded Britain already had bases on the east coast as well as across the Channel. These were refurbished seemingly in the early third century and, soon after, supplemented by a new type of coastal fort.

Strategically the east coast of Britain contained three

points of weakness when under attack: the Thames estuary,
the Wash and the Humber. Consequently the new forts
were placed to cover the approaches of the two most
southerly points, at Reculver on the north coast of Kent and
at Brancaster on the north coast of Norfolk. The forts, which
were the forerunners of a much more extensive coastal
defence system later known as the Saxon Shore, were larger
than normal auxiliary forts and probably contained, in addition to a cavalry or infantry unit, a detachment of the fleet.
That being so they were equipped to combat raiders either at
sea, or on land, if the attackers succeeded in avoiding the
naval patrols. For a short time these extra forts, coupled with
the fleet bases already in existence, were seemingly successful in meeting the new threat. However, the increasing scale
of their operations soon demanded additional measures and
by the end of the third century the fully-fledged Saxon
Shore system was in operation. But that lies beyond the
scope of this book.

In sum, therefore, it can be seen that, although the
Romans were in many ways remarkably successful in their
military campaigns in Britain, they had their share of
failures. Some would claim that the successes were strictly
circumscribed and that all their failures can be compounded
into one: solely their apparent inability or disinclination to
conquer the whole island. In addition we have to conclude
this chapter on a note of failure, but failure not so much in
the British provinces as in the central institutions of the
empire. The middle part of the third century saw increasing
disorder caused by civil wars, invasions and rampant monetary inflation. Yet from all these, Britain remained largely
immune, protected on the one hand by the Channel, from
barbarian invasions of the type which did so much damage
to the provinces of Germany and Gaul, and on the other by
the secure northern frontier. The nature of the internal disturbances can perhaps be best illustrated by the position of
Britain at the time when this narrative must cease. In
AD 259, Postumus rebelled against the emperor Gallienus
and amalgamated the British, Spanish and Gaulish
provinces into an independent Gallic empire which survived for fifteen years. But we might suspect that it made
little political difference to the population of Britain, whose
main concern, alike with the rest of the Roman world, was
probably with a rapidly mounting inflation and rising cost of
living.

## Chapter five

# 'Pax Romana' — the benefits for Britain

The firm establishment of a romanised British province took place gradually over the best part of a century. Even after that period further, but relatively more minor, changes occurred and it should not be forgotten that the whole empire was continually subject to a process closely akin to organic growth; periods of complete stability tended to last for comparatively short terms. In Britain, the resemblance to a Roman province began to appear when areas were released from military control and handed over to local authorities organised from among the indigenous population. At first these were few and largely confined to the south-east, but, as the army advanced northwards and westwards, so others followed, until in the early second century almost all the lowland areas had been constituted into sixteen *civitates*, mostly formed from the original Iron Age tribal units. These groups, together with the three superimposed colonies of Roman army veterans at Colchester, Gloucester and Lincoln, formed the backbone of a civilian local government. The process which we today describe as romanisation partly preceded, but mostly followed in its wake.

Nevertheless, the process had, in fact, begun in a small way in the century between Caesar's expeditions and the Claudian invasion. In that time many people living in south-eastern Britain would have become familiar with pottery and metalwork imported from Gaul and other provinces. It might be claimed that they consequently became fitter and more ready to absorb the much greater technical knowledge, which they had so far lacked, and with which they came into abrupt contact after AD 43. The advances in technical skills which then appeared were mainly connected with building construction, and should be added to the newly-acquired ability to make the better-quality and more varied tools that such skills required. But among the less solid benefits must be rated those that flowed from the more peaceful conditions enjoyed after AD 43, such as greater levels of productivity, increased opportunities for making profits from trading, better communications and a better monetary system in which small change was available for

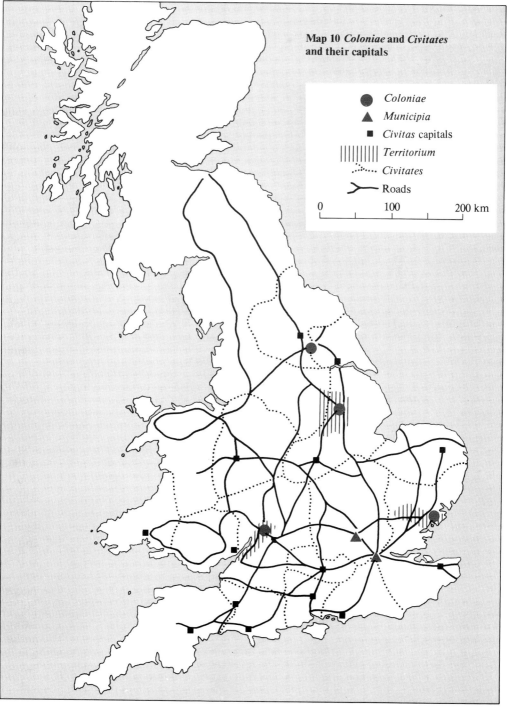

Map 10 *Coloniae* and *Civitates*
and their capitals

Coloniae
Municipia
*Civitas* capitals
Territorium
Civitates
Roads

0          100          200 km

transactions of low value, so giving rise to a more flexible system of exchange. In turn, these encouraged the development of a more civilised way of life, with improved housing, at any rate for the upper classes, their slaves and servants, and the provision of many amenities which were to be shared by a far wider range of people.

Let it be said at once, however, that the acquirement of a romanised life-style by the people of Britain was an almost entirely voluntary process, entered into freely by those who so wished and equally freely rejected by others. Little or no compulsion was employed, or, indeed, was needed and, while encouragement was sometimes given by the Roman provincial administration, financial help was seldom forthcoming.

Central to this process, to begin with, were the embryonic towns, although it must be remembered that the first real, if restricted, view of romanised life that many Britons obtained was from the army. In the early days after the conquest it was in their midst and would have provided their introduction to many of the new processes. Moreover, deliberate examples of urbanisation were often manufactured in new provinces by the discharge of large bodies of legionaries, perhaps up to 2,000 or more in strength, and usually at the end of a major period of campaigning, who would be given plots of land for both development and agriculture in a newly-designated town and its surrounding area. These towns were called *coloniae* and were given the rights of self-governing communities, according to laws set out in a charter. Caesar founded a number in southern Gaul in the province of Narbonensis, while in other western provinces, Augustus founded more in north Italy and Spain. Their establishment can, therefore, be seen as part of a deliberate imperial policy towards the provinces. In Britain the first colony was founded at Colchester in AD 49, by a discharge of soldiers probably from Legio XX, and use was made of the recently abandoned legionary fortress. This formed the nucleus of the new town, around which land was added for agricultural purposes; each soldier received a plot inside the town and another in the territory attached, the areas being related to his rank. It is also likely that room was made for some members of the native population. The town was governed by a council, usually consisting of about one hundred members, who, in order to qualify for election, had to possess a certain level of wealth or property. There were also four, and sometimes six, executive officers who carried out the day-to-day administration. The senior pair acted as justices in the courts and had various other civic duties; the junior pair were in charge of public works, while, if there were six, the remaining pair were expected to look after the financial affairs of the town.

Tacitus tells us a certain amount about the earliest town at Colchester in his account of the Boudiccan rebellion. He refers to a theatre, to a council chamber, to statues of Victory and to the absence of defences. The latter reference is odd for it would seem from modern investigations that the fortifications of the original legionary fortress still stood round the *colonia*. It may be that Tacitus did not deem them worthy of mention and was thinking more in terms of masonry. Some of the first houses have also been excavated and would appear to be quite simple buildings, with the walls often constructed of unbaked mud brick, a sensible compromise in an area where good building stone did not occur, and one which was commonly employed in southern and eastern Mediterranean countries.

The pride of the new administration was also placed at Colchester: the temple of the Imperial Cult, dedicated to Claudius, founder of the British province. Built on an heroic scale, it even excited comment in Rome. It appears to have lain outside the town to the east and was situated in its own splendid, colonnaded court. The manufacture of a state religion by the emperor Augustus was done to give a degree of cohesion to non-Roman provincials in an otherwise religiously heterogeneous empire. The central theme was the oath of loyalty to the emperor and his ancestors which assumed aspects of both civil and religious importance. Such a concept was most easily introduced into the eastern provinces, where the equation of a living person with a deity had for long been the custom. In the west, however, it seems to have had a mixed reception. It was successful in Gaul where the combined centre for the three north-western provinces was situated at Lyons, but was less successful, apparently, in Germany. In Britain, despite its remarkable introduction, it does not seem to have been popular at first; later, however, native resistance was reduced and there are indications of a fairly wide acceptance. But at Colchester, the first efforts of the colonists were to no avail; all went up in flames in the Boudiccan rebellion, and evidence for the conflagration is, from time to time, uncovered in excavations.

Colchester was not, however, the only veteran *colonia* founded in Britain. In the years following the military campaigns of Agricola, when Britain appears to have been peaceful, further discharges from the army were made and towns established at Lincoln and Gloucester. Once again,

75

vacant legionary fortresses were re-used and it is interesting to observe at Gloucester the rows of terrace houses for the colonists which replaced the lines of very similarly-planned barrack blocks. By the end of the first century, therefore, Britain possessed three 'model' towns to act as a stimulus for the building activities of the native population.

Urbanisation at native level started only slowly. Verulamium and Canterbury seem to have been the first to show some degree of ordered development and planning, and at the former, which was perhaps one of the original strongholds of a Roman ally, it would seem that military architects and surveyors had been lent to instruct the people in the new building methods. The planning and construction of one block of shops had a distinctly barrack-like appearance. At Verulamium, also, the Boudiccan rebellion was a serious set-back to the growing town, from which it did not fully recover for well over a decade. Nevertheless we must be cautious in such an assessment. Plots remained vacant for a long time in many towns of England after the bombing of the last war, but that did not mean that the towns themselves were not prosperous and viable communities.

But although the start of urbanisation was perhaps a little uncertain, the seeds of a much wider blossoming were being sown in the villages which were beginning to grow and prosper round the many forts of the Midlands and south-west in the first few decades after the invasion. It was in these that the native Iron Age peoples, till now largely unaccustomed to sophisticated urban life, began to learn something of the processes by which they could achieve it. They became schooled in a small way in the methods of local government and started to appreciate the much greater market economy which towns and villages provided. Forts represented a continuous demand and provided a stable market for the sale of surplus production, so that farmers and manufacturers would have been encouraged to increase the surplus to their greater profit. Larger profits meant more money to spend on the much wider range of goods and services which were becoming available, many probably brought at first by foreign traders. But for the full flowering of urbanisation in Britain, something more was needed.

The opportunity arose when the military advance into Wales and the north was resumed in the early 70s. The removal of almost every garrison in a wide band stretching from the south-west up to Lincolnshire required the establishment of a suitable system of local government to replace the military administration. This was achieved, as before in

Gaul and in south-east Britain, by using the Iron Age tribal structure, each suitable tribe being constituted a *civitas*. The management was placed in the hands of those members of the tribal aristocracy who were acceptable to the provincial administration and, as far as we know from the evidence available from both Britain and other western provinces, was modelled on the system used in the chartered towns. Consequently, there would have been a council and two pairs of magistrates in each. Variations were, nevertheless, allowed on occasion to take account of local customs and nomenclature.

Each established *civitas* also needed a centre — a capital — from which the administration could work. The site for it would normally have been chosen from among the military villages in, or near, which lived the greatest proportion of the tribal leaders. Thus, the village so selected formed the nucleus for the town which was to grow in its place, and this phase of development saw the foundation of nine towns that ranked as civitas capitals. But the rate of progress within them was uneven, demonstrating yet again the voluntary nature of the process, and we find that some of the newly designated towns developed rapidly while others lagged behind. It also happened to be an age when, over much of the empire, local government was investing in major public buildings, such as the integrated forum and basilica complex. By around the turn of the first and second centuries, Cirencester, Silchester, Winchester, Exeter, Verulamium and possibly some others were well on the way to achieving the desired quota of public buildings, while others, such as, Leicester, Wroxeter and Caistor-by-Norwich, did not reach the same peak until almost the middle of the second century. Further distinctions between individual towns can also be detected. There is considerable variation in size, ranging from about 101 ha for Cirencester to about 44 ha for Leicester and down to about 17 ha for Caerwent, and the area of the town is usually reflected in the size of its public buildings. No two fora or bath-houses are alike in their planning; even such basically simple buildings as amphitheatres show differences. There are also unexpected surprises; some of the most sophisticated, Mediterranean-style, private houses are to be found in the little town of Caerwent, on the fringe of the civilised area of Roman Britain. Indeed the only common factors to be observed among most towns were probably the planned, rectangular system of streets which the majority possessed, the siting of the forum and basilica at the main cross-roads in the town centre, the existence, eventually, of the normal run of public buildings and works, such as forum, bath-house, water supply and amphitheatre, and the use of the town centre for commercial premises; there the similarities end, and there are even exceptions in these criteria.

It seems clear, therefore, that the construction of towns was left largely to private enterprise, even if, in the early days, it was supported by the loan of military architects. So we can demonstrate once again the lack of compulsion, and correspondingly the degree of voluntary acceptance, practised by the provincial government on the one hand and by the local inhabitants on the other. There is evidence, as we have already seen, for practical help being provided by the former for the latter, but mainly we must conclude that these towns were constructed, and paid for, by the native Britons for their own use. Had this not been so, we would surely have detected a much more rigid, standardised pattern. Moreover, no government, ancient or modern, has yet successfully devised a way of compelling people to spend their own money on buildings, goods and services which they do not want. In order to achieve that end the money has first to be taken in some form of tax or levy and then spent on these unwanted objectives by a government agency, specially set up for the purpose; no such agency ever existed for the specific purpose of building towns in Roman Britain, or, for that matter, in any other part of the empire. Indeed the whole provincial administration taken together would have scarcely been large enough to do so. Moreover, it frequently had more important work to attend to.

If these towns were, therefore, built by the native inhabitants for their own use, one of the first questions to arise is how were they paid for. The laying-out of a regular network of streets on a nearly virgin site, the construction of aqueducts and sewers and of massive public buildings, would have demanded considerable expenditure. In modern terms it would probably have cost several million pounds per town. Yet local taxes were minimal, and revenue was normally raised from duty on goods passing the boundary, from fees paid by office-holders on election, rents for public land, fines levied in the courts, sale of water from the aqueduct and personal gifts. But even taken together, all these sources would, seemingly, have been insufficient to raise more than annual income, when it was large capital resources that were required. Admittedly, as in the rest of the empire, wealthy individuals could donate to the community some handsome gift, such as a new stage for a theatre, on election to the tribal council or to a magistracy, but he would have been a rich man indeed who could afford, without the risk of bankruptcy, to give a complete forum and basilica.

There are now, as there were in antiquity, many ways for local authorities to raise capital sums of money. It can be raised by straightforward borrowing, and we know from Tacitus that, in the period immediately after the Roman invasion, large sums were loaned to Britain's leaders by Roman money-lenders. Indeed, it was the attempt at a too-hasty retrieval by those same lenders that contributed to the Boudiccan rebellion. We may suspect, however, that, having once burnt their fingers, the tribal rulers would not be too ready to approach the same sources again. Another way in which to raise capital is by the sale of communally-owned land. Although it is virtually impossible to demonstrate this method in action in Roman Britain, there are differences in the distribution patterns of villas round some towns, which may indicate that some *civitates* were more prepared to sell land to private buyers than some others. This is most noticeable if we compare the areas around Cirencester and Canterbury. At the former, the town lay in the centre of an area dominated by many villas, with the exception of a small inner zone, free of villas, round the town. Round Canterbury, villas were very few in number, in contrast to the greater number in the western part of the tribal area. It would be rash to press this argument much further at present, but, if villas are taken normally to represent private farms, then we might assume that there was far more land in private ownership in the territory of Dobunni than in that of the Cantii, possibly pointing to a greater readiness to sell by the former tribe. Could this be the reason why Cirencester is both larger and apparently more richly-endowed than almost all other civitas capitals?

Yet another way to raise money is to capitalise on natural resources, which can range from timber to minerals. Although some tribal areas contained extensive deposits of the ores of iron, lead, copper, tin and silver, only iron ore could apparently continue to be worked freely by the natives. Some form of imperial control may well have been exercised over the rest. There were seemingly no quick profits to be made, therefore, in this sector of the economy, while other minerals such as stone, lime, clay, gravel and sand, all probably much in demand, were too readily available to bring a large return, although undoubtedly contributing a measure of financial gain. Timber was, however, another matter. All building work requires its quota of timber, whether for walls, roofs, floors or even scaffolding. Moreover, in the early period of urbanisation in Britain, only public buildings were constructed of masonry, most privately-owned property being built with timber frames. In the early fourth century, a good-sized fir tree may have fetched as much as the wheat crop from 5 ha of land, so that the felling of mature woodland, which at the time abounded in Britain, could have released considerable capital sums, while at the same time it would have provided the timber needed for building operations and cleared more land for agricultural purposes. All-round benefits would thus have accrued.

The last method of raising money is by seeking grants from the central government, which in the case of the Roman empire was usually done by obtaining a remission of taxes or the cancellation of a tax debt. It is not easy to show that emperors either remitted taxes or gave other grants to indigent urban communities in Britain, although they certainly did so in a number of provinces, some being more generous than others. It is perhaps, therefore, not entirely coincidence that the two great periods of urban expansion in Britain occurred during the principates of Vespasian and Titus and Hadrian. The imperial biographer Suetonius notes that many statues of Titus were to be observed in Britain and Germany, a fact normally attributed to the emperor having commanded a legion in Britain and having been governor of Lower Germany before succeeding his father in Rome. It is perhaps understandable why Germany should have so many statues, a governor being an important man. But why should commemorative statues have been erected to a mere legionary commander in sufficient numbers to be noteworthy in Britain? It was customary throughout the empire to honour major benefactors by erecting statues to them in public places. Were those of Titus, therefore, an indication that, through his governor, Agricola, and after he had become emperor, he helped some of the towns of Britain by the remission of taxes, so that they could equip themselves with the visible symbols of local government in the form of public buildings? If so, not all towns then benefited, for, as we have already seen some, although founded in the first century AD, were not provided with their major buildings until the principate of Hadrian, or even later. This emperor visited Britain, as well as many other provinces; he was also greatly interested in encouraging building schemes. It is reasonable to suppose that, having assessed the situation on the spot, he provided further financial aid in Britain.

The establishment of an urban-based society undoubtedly brought large benefits to many people, but equally disadvantages to others. The tribal leaders were virtually tied to the towns once they became magistrates or councillors, for there were laws governing their place of residence. If, therefore, they possessed country estates, the day-to-day running would have been placed in the hands of a manager or bailiff. Nevertheless, their estates will have gained by the provision of a continuous market for their products in the new towns and villages, which required to be fed. The increased prosperity must in time also have

**36** Fragmentary inscription (*CIL* VI, 967) from the forum of Trajan in Rome recording the cancellation of a huge tax debt owed to the treasury. Fully restored it would have read:

[*S(enatus) P(opulus) Q(ue) R(omanus) Imp(eratore) Caesari Divi Traiani Parthici f(ilio) Divi Nervae Nepoti*] *Traiano* [*Hadriano Augusto Pont(ifici)*] *Max(imo) Tr*[*ib(unicia) Pot(estate) II Co(n)s(uli) II*] *qui primus omn*[*ium principum et s*[*olus remittend*[*o sestertium novies mil*]*es centena m*[*ilia n(ummum) debitum fiscis non praesentes tantum cives suos sed et posteros eorum praestitit hac liberalitate securos*

'The Roman senate and people to the Emperor Caesar Trajan Hadrian Augustus, son of the deified Trajan Parthicus, grandson of the deified Nerva, chief priest, holder of the tribunician power for the second year, twice consul, the first and only one of the emperors to cancel 900,100,000 sesterces owed to the treasury and by this liberality to render not only the citizens now living but also their descendants free from worry.'

reached even remote country dwellers, who could also take advantage of the availability of a wider range of manufactured goods, ranging from pottery to iron tools.

Principally, therefore, the new towns and villages acted as marketing and servicing centres for catchment areas which varied in size according to their situations. To this extent we can envisage a pattern developing in which major towns, like the *coloniae* or civitas capitals, possessed a wider sphere of influence than the nearest minor settlements or villages, the latter providing a much narrower range of services over a smaller area. As today, most villages could probably provide, in a single, or small number of shops, the basic essentials of life for their inhabitants. But the country folk who depended on the village for these, and even the villagers themselves, might have been forced to make the longer journey to the nearest major town for their more sophisticated requirements, since the towns provided a more comprehensive range of goods and services. As, in many cases, the major town was the centre of the communication system for a given area, this will not have been too onerous a task. Equally, it is possible that itinerant merchants made their rounds of the countryside, as well as attending the main urban markets. So in time, we might expect that knowledge of the new technologies, in addition to its products, could have spread to even the most humble rural dwelling. But studies of the distribution of certain types of pottery show that this is perhaps a too optimistic view. The largest quantities are usually found within comparatively short distances of main roads, indicating that, for this common commodity, penetration into the deeper countryside was not always achieved.

There is much evidence for the goods and services provided by towns both for their own inhabitants and for those people in the neighbouring countryside who were dependent on them. Shops were normally numerous in the commercial centre of a town, and may have been privately-owned and managed, or run by a slave or freedman for an absentee owner. In addition, in the major towns such as the civitas capitals, there were public buildings devoted to trade such as the forum, or a separate market hall, while in the smaller towns and villages, an open space was sometimes left in the centre to act as a market place, in which stalls could be erected on market days. It is, of course, often difficult to show what trade or business was carried on in any shop. Nevertheless, hardware shops selling samian pottery and glassware have been found at Colchester, the stock having been partly preserved when the building was burnt in the Boudiccan rebellion. A butchers' market has been suggested for a public building near the forum at Cirencester, where the refuse from boned meat was buried in pits beneath the floors. In one block at Verulamium there were shops occupied by a wine-merchant and by manufacturing smiths. A goldsmith in the centre of London had a large establishment where the metal was refined, while a smith at Silchester was recovering silver from its alloys with other metals in a cupellation furnace. Blacksmiths were probably ubiquitous in both large and small towns and there is evidence for their activities at Silchester, Verulamium and Great Chesterford, while the tombstone of another came from a cemetery outside York. A sculptor had his workshop at either Cirencester or Bath, and the latter site has also produced evidence for a jeweller carving semi-precious stones. Catterick, Verulamium and Colchester all had manufacturing bronze-smiths. Even the comparatively minor town at Norton, close to the fort at Malton in east Yorkshire, possessed a gold-smith. Workshops for the manufacture of second-century mosaic pavements have also been suggested for a number of towns, such as Cirencester and Verulamium or Colchester.

It is even more difficult to show the presence of shops devoted to the manufacture and sale of organic materials, since they will only seldom survive in the soil, but a leather factory may be indicated for a building at Alcester. A shoeshop may likewise be suggested for an extramural building at Cirencester, as it produced a large number of hob-nails. Presumably there were in each major town shops dealing in cloth, fruit, vegetables, woodwork and leather, but it is almost impossible to prove their presence. There must also have been a number of restaurants, inns and probably brothels.

If economic factors were important elements in the com-

**37** Restored shop in Corinium Museum, Cirencester, of a mosaic worker. Most of the materials used for mosaics were derived from different coloured stones or brick, but sometimes both coloured glass and samian fragments were employed

position of towns, there were also some in which administration played almost as crucial a role in their life. As centres of local government for either a colonial territory or a civitas capital they would have a wide catchment area attracting people who ranged from the administrators themselves to those having business with the offices or courts. Once there they would obviously make use of the other facilities offered, which would be developed accordingly, sometimes perhaps combining business with purchasing or

**38** (a) Section of the timber quay which lined the north bank of the Thames at London, stretching from about London Bridge to the Tower of London. The box-like construction was anchored by vertical posts driven into the foreshore; the whole structure was presumably furnished with a deck of planks.
(b) Reconstruction drawing of a length of the quay

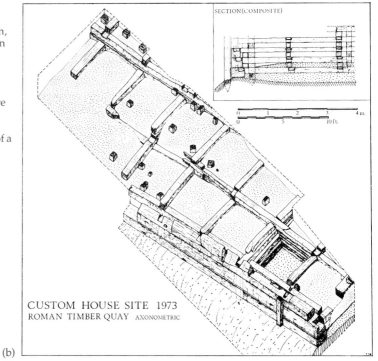

SECTION(COMPOSITE)

CUSTOM HOUSE SITE 1973
ROMAN TIMBER QUAY AXONOMETRIC

with pleasure. The same would be true of the lesser sites in a descending degree.

There was one major site where both these factors were enhanced: London. This town seems at first to have been developed as the result of spontaneous economic growth, so much so that Tacitus, in his account of the Boudiccan rebellion, refers to its large population, consisting mostly of merchants. Its economic strength cannot, therefore, be doubted, especially as, by the late first century, it had become the provincial capital, seat of the governor, and the base for the financial management of the province, which was placed in the hands of the procurator. To London came traders from all parts of the empire; its long quay, stretching from near London Bridge to the Tower, will seldom have been idle, and, although imported goods are known to have travelled direct to other parts of the province, London probably handled the lion's share. It is not surprising, therefore, that it became the largest, and probably the richest town in Britain. We cannot be certain if it was promoted to chartered status, the first stage of which would have been the intermediate one of *municipium*. But the indications are there to show that it was almost certainly a self-governing community from a comparatively early age, so that promotion must seem likely.

We have considered, so far together, all urban settlements, no matter their size and status, from the *coloniae* at the top to the minor towns and villages below. The only distinctions drawn so far have been the legal status of the chartered towns on the one hand and the more restricted services provided by the minor sites on the other. But it must be admitted that it is extremely difficult to differentiate between many of the sites in the middle of the scale. We have a basis for so doing in the economic criteria mentioned above, but, unfortunately, it is almost impossible to say that such-and-such a town contained a greater variety of shops and services than such-and-such a village ten kilometres distant. We would need far more detailed knowledge about these sites than we have at present, for not only would all the shops and factories have to be identified but additionally we would have to be able to show in what goods they dealt, and what level of trade was enjoyed by them.

There is, however, a possible way round such a difficulty, because a wide economic base in a town is sometimes matched by the amenities which the place offers, and which are not to be found in the lesser sites. Fortunately amenities often require buildings or structures of a specific nature, which can be readily identified by their plan or their fittings.

Thus the provision of special administrative buildings, a public bath-house, a supply of running water, good sewers, a theatre or amphitheatre, colonnaded or arcaded streets and good quality housing, are all indicative of a fairly high level of enjoyment on the part of the inhabitants. Happily, in the Roman world, we can distinguish those sites which possess all these amenities as representing the peak of urbanisation. Below, however, there can be no clear-cut distinctions, but only a gradually-descending series in which those in the middle possess some amenities while those at the bottom have none that are detectable. As yet it is almost impossible to say at precisely what point on the scale we stop calling such sites towns; attempts to do so have created some invidious distinctions and have only manufactured more difficulties than can be readily solved.

The amenities which have so far been categorised are normally to be found in the major towns of Britain, such as the *coloniae*, *municipia* and civitas capitals. Other sites often possess some, if not all, while at the bottom of the list there is a series of settlements which do not appear to have any of the representative buildings. These might justifiably be called villages, since they seem to provide only the most basic services for their inhabitants, but to do so is perhaps a little unwise since so few have been even partly, let alone fully, excavated.

The amenities which can be readily identified have already been listed. Apart from private housing, most would have been provided by the local authority for the benefit of the inhabitants. First and foremost would probably have been the forum and basilica, used not only as offices and law-courts by the administration but also providing accommodation for shopkeepers and itinerant traders who could set up their stalls in the colonnades or the piazza. Important also were the streets, which in many towns, as with Lincoln, Verulamium and Cirencester, were flanked by colonnades or arcades to give protection both to shoppers and to shopkeepers' wares displayed in the open-fronted buildings behind. The streets themselves were cambered and metalled and usually provided with drainage gulleys to carry away water. Nevertheless constant traffic quickly wore out the surfaces which often degenerated into fine dust or mud according to the weather; as a result repairs were frequent. Consequently the street levels were gradually raised in height, sometimes causing considerable annoyance to householders or shopkeepers who found that water or mud drained into their premises.

The most important social building was undoubtedly the

bath-house which would possess rooms maintained at different temperatures by means of hypocausts, or underfloor heating. Many were of considerable size and splendour, that at Wroxeter even containing the unusual feature of an outdoor swimming bath. There, also, the walls were in part lined with mosaic, while in others veneers of imported marbles were similarly used. Most contained either an open area, or a covered hall, which could be used for exercise.

The baths also housed the main public lavatory which was flushed by the outflow of waste water. As a result large sewers were required which sometimes communicated, as at Lincoln, with a considerable system underlying the main streets. A bath-house, therefore, required great volumes of running water, supplied from the town's aqueduct. It can be shown that almost every major, as well as some minor, towns were supplied with water in this manner, the aqueducts normally tapping a source which was so situated that the water was not only unpolluted but could also be led to the town by gravity flow in a pipe or ditch. Only at Lincoln was there, seemingly, a more complicated system where the water had to be carried to a hill-top town. In most cases, once the supply of water reached the town it was distri-

**39** View of the early fourth-century bath-house at Catterick during excavation. This building succeeded two earlier bath-houses, but was never completed

buted, either in pipes of lead, wood or ceramic, or by conduits constructed of stone, to both public and private users.

Special buildings devoted to entertainment were also constructed in many towns and formed part of the amenities they provided. Foremost in Britain was the amphitheatre, an elliptical building with a central arena surrounded by raked banks of seats. Various types of blood-letting sports or spectacles were performed in them, such as gladiatorial

**40** Maumbury Rings, Dorchester. The town's amphitheatre was built on the site of a Neolithic henge monument, the banks of which were supplemented to carry the seating round the arena. The amphitheatre is unusual in having only one arena entrance and the structural elements were composed entirely of wood

combats, or fights between man and beast, or beast and beast, as well as certain forms of public execution. The majority were large enough to accommodate not only the entire population of the town but probably also a high proportion of country visitors. The theatre, on the other hand, was altogether less popular in Britain; few are known and at least two were associated with temples. Normally, they were D-shaped buildings with the stage set along the straight side and with ranks of seats round the circumference. In north-west Europe, however, a compromise was sometimes adopted and the theatre was so constructed that it could double as an amphitheatre if the need arose. The theatre at Verulamium, closely related to an adjacent temple, was planned in this manner and was almost circular in shape. In these circumstances it seems very likely that it was the religious, or semi-religious, spectacles performed in it that demanded the extra space in the arena, in addition to a raised stage, and it may be that it was the nature of these performances associated with Celtic cults that dictated the planning of the building, and not the need to economise by conflating two buildings into one. When not connected with a temple, however, the theatre was used for mimes, panto-mimes and recitations, a type of amusement which was not perhaps very popular in Britain.

The third main form of public entertainment in the Roman world was horse- and chariot-racing, which took place in the circus, a long rectangular building with one rounded end. No such structures have yet been identified in Britain, but it would be surprising, knowing the Celtic love of both horse-racing and gambling, had the sport not been prac-tised. There is however, a suggestive building at Wroxeter which seems to be connected with a nearby temple, whose deities included an equine content. Ritual horse-racing may, therefore, have been part of the cult practices.

Among the lesser amenities of the major towns must also be rated the provision of a far wider range of temples, representative of many different cults. Among them were both classical and native varieties, which were often syn-thesised in a mixture of religious thoughts, so that Minerva might be equated with Brigantia in northern England or with Sulis at Bath. Thus the religious repertoire of major towns was more extensive than that of the lesser settlements which might only boast a single temple dedicated to a par-ticular native deity. Consequently, the inhabitants of the larger towns had a greater choice in their dedications, so covering a wider range of human activities.

The higher standard of private housing can also be con-sidered as an amenity, although it was some time before the peak of luxury was reached around the middle of the second century. Even then houses were still occasionally being con-structed with timber frames, which precluded the ultimate refinement of heating by hypocaust. Nevertheless such houses could still contain first-class mosaics and wall paintings and it is possible to distinguish, in many cases, between the rooms occupied by the family and those of the slaves or servants. Many houses which started from humble beginnings grew to considerable size with any number up to four wings, arranged around an inner courtyard or garden. Some even possessed their own small, private, bath suites, while occasionally some were also connected to the town's water supply.

Whether protection can be classed as an amenity is an

arguable point, since it is not impossible that some towns, such as the British *coloniae*, were fortified for the sake of appearance, rather than for protection. Nevertheless, the provision of defences for whatever purpose, albeit only a bank and ditch, or a more elaborate system of masonry walls, gates and turrets, must have given the inhabitants a comfortable feeling of safety. By the end of the second century most major towns, together with some minor ones,

**41** Fourth-century town-houses at the Beeches, Cirencester. The further contained a fine mosaic, manufactured locally, with an illustration of a hare at the centre

had been given at least an earth bank and a ditch, while some, as with London, Colchester, Lincoln and Gloucester, had been fully or partly equipped with masonry fortifications. It would seem that the intention had been to provide masonry defences for all those sites then fortified, but the suddenly arising need for a speedy completion required a compromise; hence the different methods of construction. However, by the end of the third century those towns with earth banks had been strengthened by the addition of stone walls, while some, not previously fortified at all, had been equally protected. There is a direct comparison here to be drawn between the towns of Britain and of Gaul and Germany. In the latter provinces, the serious barbarian invasions which took place soon after the middle of the third century caught many towns unawares and with no defences; many suffered badly, and when shortly afterwards walls were erected, they frequently enclosed only a small part of the original area. Britain, on the other hand, was not touched by those troubles. Had it been, the towns would probably have fared less badly, since most had already been protected as a precautionary measure. Had those precautions not then been taken it is unlikely that defences would have been built later, so that when, in the late fourth and fifth centuries, external forces began to attack Britain,

the towns would have suffered as badly as did those in Gaul at an earlier date. So the precautions, even though they were not needed at the time, paid eventual dividends and preserved the towns of Britain longer than might otherwise have been the case.

In addition to the major towns and to what we might call 'general purpose' minor settlements, which should include the military villages of the north and Wales, there were a number of smaller sites that grew on an altogether narrower base. These were the sites which had a specific function, more often than not related to religious or industrial factors. Two of the most obviously connected with religion were the two spas at Bath and Buxton. The site at Bath is comparatively well known and at its centre was a large sanctuary with a classical styled temple dedicated jointly to Sulis and Minerva. The Celtic deity gave its name to the site: Aquae

42 Aerial photograph showing cropmarks caused by buildings and other structures in the minor town on Watling Street at Whilton Lodge (Bannaventa). This town was reputedly the birthplace of St Patrick. Although the boundaries clearly continued into the lighter coloured field in the top centre, that part was unfortunately destroyed by gravel digging before excavations could take place

Sulis. Connected to the religious enclosure was the main hot spring and the various and extensive bathing establishments which led from it. The town was ultimately deemed important enough to be given walls, and it is possible that part of its overall function was as a military convalescent centre. Although little is known about the rest of the town, it may be assumed that it primarily served the large number of pilgrims who visited the site, and secondarily, perhaps, the belt of rich villas which eventually grew in its neighbourhood. Altogether less is known of Buxton. That it was a site closely akin in nature to Bath is given by its name: Aquae Arnemetiae. Hot springs exist, even today, but nothing is known of the Roman bathing establishment. Another site which seems to have been connected with a religious sanctuary is Springhead in north-west Kent, but its development was on a much more modest scale.

Among the places which seem primarily to have been associated with industry might be mentioned Charterhouse-in- Mendip, where there were extensive lead mines. At first the metal was extracted under military supervision, denoting the probable existence of an imperial estate. Later, however, a sizeable settlement grew, complete with an amphitheatre, and, with the eventual cessation of army control, it is likely that the mines were leased to concession-aires, either companies or wealthy individuals; their presence is, in fact, attested as early as the late first century. Other sites which seem to have been closely connected with extractive industries are Kenchester and Weston-under-Penyard, both in Herefordshire. They seem to have served the iron-ore mines of the Forest of Dean, and Kenchester became sufficiently important to be fortified. Similarly, Mancetter, on the main road, Watling Street, near Nuneaton, seems to have been the service centre for extensive potteries, stretching for several square kilometres around it. Wilderspool, in Cheshire, on the other hand, not only made pots, but also contributed to the metal- and glass-working industries.

In sum, therefore, there were many nucleated settlements ranging widely in both size and status; the significant difference between those at the top and those at the bottom would seem to be the level of amenities offered, not only for the local inhabitants, but also for the people in the countryside round about. The larger the site and the greater the variety of amenities offered, then the greater the area it could serve. As already noted, there is no difficulty in referring to those at the top of the scale as towns, but it becomes almost impossible within the boundaries of our present knowledge

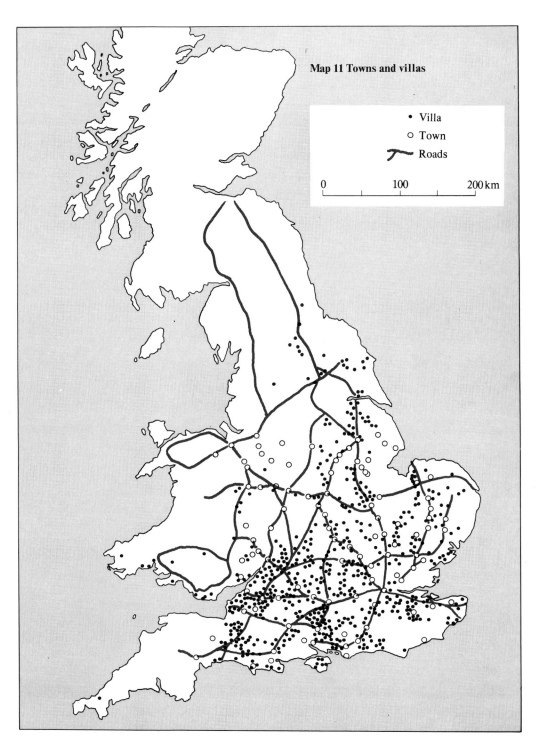

**Map 11 Towns and villas**

- • Villa
- ○ Town
- ⌒ Roads

0          100         200 km

to distinguish between a town and a village in the middle orders of the hierarchy, as, indeed it sometimes is today.

The countryside which was served by these settlements during the Roman period in Britain shows an equal diversity. In most areas, the process of romanisation was slower than in the corresponding towns, while there remained zones beyond the lowlands in which Roman culture and technology was, at best, acquired but fitfully. From this we can infer that towns were an essential requirement for the full development of the countryside in a romanised manner. A glance at a distribution map of Roman villas shows how intimately they were connected to the towns and villages; where none existed, neither were there more than isolated villas, such as that near Illogan in Cornwall. In the West Country, farm residences remained much as they had been in the Iron Age, the extent of romanisation being usually limited to the use of better-quality pottery and metalwork.

We can consider, therefore, that the villa was an essential element of a largely romanised countryside, although here, as with towns, there was also a hierarchy, with, at the top, the large, splendid, first-century examples at Fishbourne, Eccles and Angmering, through the middle range of comfortable houses, such as mid-second-century Ditchley, High Wycombe and Park Street, to the small cottage type represented by the earliest buildings at Park Street and Welwyn. Moreover, it can sometimes be shown, or suspected, that villas replaced earlier, Iron Age farms. What produced the transformation? Undoubtedly it must have been partly the dissemination of the techniques of new construction, which were probably first observed in the towns and then applied to country houses. But the development of an Iron Age farmhouse into a villa also required capital investment, sometimes on a considerable scale. Such capital will mainly have accrued from the profits on the sale of marketable produce to the towns and villages and to the army. It may, therefore, have taken some time for a farmer to have accumulated the necessary capital, which might possibly account for the slower pace of development in the countryside. First would have to come an increase in production, brought about partly by the demands of the Roman tax-collector, and necessitating the clearance of more land for cultivation or pasture. To help this process there became available a wider range of new and better-quality farm implements, such as the heavier plough with mould-board and coulter, the iron-bound wooden spade, more efficient sickles and scythes, larger and more robust grub axes and saws, which enabled both the clearance of forest and scrub to take place more easily and the ploughing of heavier soils. As already hinted earlier the felling of woodland might itself provide a useful capital return. But as the clearance increased, so greater would have become the surplus of production which could be used to satisfy other markets. The growth of profits would ultimately have led to the accumulation of capital, since probably not all of the annual yield would have been needed for the ordinary running expenses

43 Aerial photograph of the exposed area of the villa at Witcombe (Glos.). The villa lies on the scarp of the Cotswolds overlooking the Severn Valley and Gloucester

of the farm. As a rough and ready guide, therefore, the size and standard of furnishing of a villa is a measure not of the size of a farm but of its profitability.

However, there are complications, of which it is wise to be aware, before using this yard-stick in a wholesale manner. Villas can represent various classes of land-using people and there are a number of permutations which can be made. They can represent the permanent domestic residences of the land-owning gentry, farming large acreages, perhaps with the help of tenants or dependants. But in the main, we might suspect that, with one or two exceptions, these arrangements were confined to the fourth century. Equally they could represent the residences of the tenant farmers. Alternatively they might be the houses of bailiffs or managers running large estates for absentee landlords, into which category we should also fit those used by the imperial procurator's men for administering imperial estates, such as the building called a *principia* at Combe Down near Bath. They could also be the houses of small-scale freeholders.

Finally, since the word villa was, and is, not always used strictly to mean a farm, they could represent the residences of those engaged in industrial enterprises, such as mineral extraction or pottery-making. So the complexities of land-ownership and use in the Roman period were probably not much less than those of today. Since our information for the period is so slight it is seldom possible to judge the relationship between one villa and its neighbours. Since, also, a

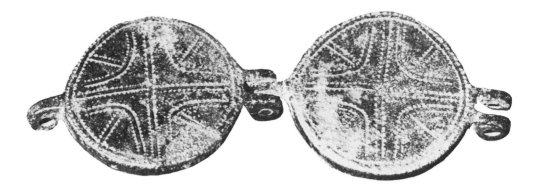

**44** Lead seal issued by the procurator of Britannia Superior and found in the *principia* at Combe Down, outside Bath. It is stamped *PBRS* for *P(rovinciae) Br(itanniae)* . *S(uperioris)*. This villa was the headquarters of an imperial estate.

market economy was functioning, estates could be bought and sold, expanded or contracted, and even sequestrated by the emperor; all were events which might produce little or no immediate visible alteration in the appearance of the villa residence at the centre, but might be important for its economic life.

In view of the foregoing assessment, it is probably right to conclude that the few early villas of substance were the properties of people already in possession of good capital resources. The palatial residence at Fishbourne, near Chichester, has been linked with the client king of the southern Atrebates, Cogidubnus, and there are many features of the building which might well justify such a conclusion, but for the fact that it was barely completed before the supposed date of his death. Less certainty attaches to the other splendid building at Eccles in west Kent, but if it is right to associate the Kentish kingdom with Adminius, as has been suggested on coin evidence, it is not impossible that it was he who built it. As the only known ally of Rome among the hostile Catuvellauni, it is more than likely that he returned to Britain in the wake of the Roman army. But such men would already be possessed of considerable fortunes, which may have been supplemented by their services in the Roman cause, and, providing the inclination was there, they could have equipped themselves with spectacular country houses in the latest fashion. The contrast comes when we consider Prasutagus, the client king of the Iceni, who, despite his supposed wealth, does not seem to have felt the need for such an outward display of pro-Roman enthusiasm, for no villa of this class or early date has yet been found in Norfolk. We must not forget, either, the possibility that these early villas were the result of the investment of foreign capital in a new province on the part of merchants, who saw the opportunity to buy themselves into the land-owning classes.

But for the larger proportion of Romano-British villas, we can probably infer that they were developed by local land-owners or tenant farmers for their own use. In most cases it was the end of the first century before Roman-style architecture replaced the native round-house, and the earliest of such buildings were usually extremely simple, often consisting of no more than a single block with, perhaps, an external corridor. Nevertheless, by the later second century many of these had become much larger, often by the addition of subsidiary wings to the original nucleus, and, although the standards were still comparatively modest when compared with the best town houses of the period, they appear to have been comfortable dwellings. Improvements can also be noted in the farm buildings, with barns and granaries constructed to house animals, cereals and equipment. A well-built, damp- and rodent-proof granary would in many ways have contributed most to the success of the establishment for, by storing the grain until mid-winter or the spring, it would have commanded a much higher price when released on to the market. Equally, sheltered stock-yards and sheep-pens, together with winter fodder crops like hay or roots, would have enabled more fresh meat to be supplied all the year round. In the Iron Age, we might suspect that there was a glut of fresh meat in the autumn when surplus stock was slaughtered because of the lack of winter feed, followed by a considerable scarcity until the following spring with only smoked, dried or salted varieties available. Economically, therefore, such buildings, together with their stock and stored crops, represented a very big advance in farming methods, leading to a much higher degree of profitability. A secondary effect would have been the introduction of a more balanced diet all the year round and consequently a healthier population.

During the third century, the countryside was touched to some degree by the political and economic uncertainty of the times. Moreover, we are as yet unable to say how the civil war at the end of the second century affected private estates in Britain. If, as in Spain, large-scale sequestrations took place, as they may well have done, the sequel for the country houses might have been serious, leading to disuse and neglect.

A number of attempts have been made recently to relate villas to their estates, ranging from simple calculations of a granary's capacity, assessed in terms of crop yields and acreages, to more detailed computations of stock holdings, cultivated areas, natural woodland and grazing. But such figures, although attractive and well worthwhile, must always be viewed with extreme caution, since they can only represent the most general picture of the farming economy of the time. Nevertheless, they are a beginning and it is only through such studies that we shall perhaps one day obtain a fuller understanding of the villa system and its related agricultural practices.

Not all farming in Britain during the Roman period was associated with villas. In a number of places in the lowland areas, such as Cranbourne Chase, the Fens, along the South Downs and elsewhere, native-style farms continued to exist during the second and third centuries. It is sometimes argued that the first two areas were imperial estates, with the inhabitants being either tenants or slaves. Such farms sometimes formed loose nucleations which, in the Fens, seldom exceeded a dozen or so individual dwellings, whereas in Wiltshire they appear as sizeable villages. On the South Downs they seem to be placed on the marginal upland grazing of the villas down on the Sussex coastal plain. It is, therefore, exceedingly difficult to explain their relative position with the villas. It may be that they represent small free-holders who possessed neither the capital, nor the means to accumulate it, to advance their station in life, or possibly they were tenants or slaves of a villa estate.

The traditional patterns survived to a greater extent in the south-west, Wales and the hill country of northern Britain. The basic farm unit in much of Devon and Cornwall remained, as in the Iron Age, an enclosed house-type known as the 'round'. They were near-circular, or sometimes sub-rectangular, enclosures containing one or more round houses. The earth banks which surrounded them were thick and stone-faced, but were unlikely to have been for defence; instead they were probably intended to provide shelter, to prevent stock and children straying far from the house, and to keep out marauding wild animals. During the Roman period, however, a characteristic development was the courtyard house, seemingly derived from the round, in which a number of rooms, mostly circular in shape, were contained within a thick outer wall and opened inwards on to a central court. Clusters of these houses formed small villages, such as that at Chysauster in Cornwall.

Similar basic farming units existed in Wales and the north, although there were a number of both regional and chronological variations. On occasion, disused hill-forts were turned into farms, such as that at Dinorben in north-east Wales, where the owner was not only practising the most up-to-date methods of farming, but was also still living in a traditional Iron Age round-house. He should, therefore, be seen as a man who, in the lowland area, would probably have aspired in time to a villa, but owing to a lack of incentive or example, or to an innate conservatism, did not do so.

There is much evidence for the fields associated with the many different types of farm. The so-called Celtic fields of the Iron Age survived in many places through the Roman period and the total area devoted to them may then well have been increased. There is also evidence in some places that fields of this type were being replaced by those of larger size, which presumably made ploughing easier with a heavier machine. In other places, notably the Fens, settlements frequently had pockets of small, rectangular enclosures, which may have been used for horticultural purposes, or for enclosing stock. Likewise, other farms such as Rockbourne, Hants., seem to have been associated with large, dyked areas that were probably cattle or sheep ranches. It is still difficult to associate the majority of villas with their cultivated areas and, although some may have continued to use Celtic fields, it is not impossible that a system of open fields was employed in many, which unfortunately leave little trace of their boundaries.

Binding both the towns and the countryside of Britain together was a system of communications far more developed than any in the Iron Age. Most of the main roads were first laid out to support the lines of military advance across England, Wales and finally Scotland, and no doubt continued to serve for the movement of troops and stores even after their upkeep was relegated to the local, civilian authorities. Lesser roads were gradually added to the main trunk system and so linked minor towns and villages with the major. But many smaller settlements and outlying farms must have continued to use meandering, unmetalled trackways. The cost of upkeep of the system was probably considerable, roads, in the absence of tar macadam, degenerating rapidly to rutted tracks after the frosts and rain of winter. Annual maintenance must, therefore, have been

45 A length of unmetalled trackway discovered during the construction of the reservoir Rutland Water. Traffic had caused some erosion of the bed rock forming a slightly hollowed way, in the bottom of which wheel-ruts can be seen. Such a track led probably from a minor road to a small farm or settlement

46 A cross-section of a carvel-built boat found at Blackfriars, London, on the north bank of the Thames, together with reconstructed models of this and the County Hall boat, in the Museum of London. The latter, from County Hall, is thought to be of Mediterranean build

necessary to repair the surfaces and to ensure the best possible drainage.

Despite the improvement in communications brought about by the construction of an adequate network, road transport always remained expensive, which must have placed severe restrictions on its use over long distances. It has been calculated that a half-tonne load carried over some 500 km would have doubled in price by the time it reached its destination. Consequently, use was made, wherever possible, of water transport. This was an ideal method for carrying heavy, bulky or fragile goods and must have been very much cheaper. Britain, as with Gaul, was favoured by an extensive river system and many natural harbours, and the degree to which they were used for transport has probably always been underestimated owing to lack of evidence. Indeed it can be shown that much of the pottery production reached its markets, often a considerable distance from the

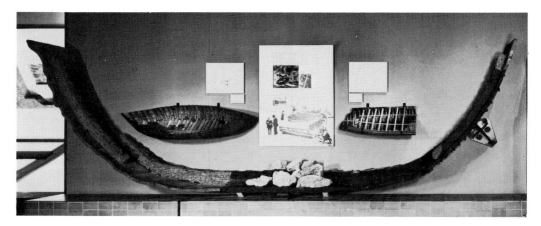

**47** Masonry relief of a large four-wheeled waggon drawn by three horses placed abreast, from the Igel monument, Trier (W. Germany)

factories, by way of river and coastwise routes, so that wares manufactured in East Anglia or the East Midlands travelled as far as the northern frontiers. It has often been claimed that the Car Dyke of the Lincolnshire and Cambridge Fens was constructed as an artificial waterway, linking the river systems of the Wash with those of the Humber. Recent research has, however, shown that this was unlikely and that it was more probably part of an extensive land reclamation scheme. Aids to navigation were few, although an army river pilot is known to have operated on the Humber and a pair of lighthouses, set one on either side of the harbour entrance, guided ships into Dover at night.

A further benefit of the *pax Romana* was the trading links made between Britain and other provinces, now sharing a largely common currency. Goods reached Britain from all parts of the empire and there were especially strong bonds with the Gaulish, Spanish and German provinces. Wine, oil, pottery, metalwork, glassware and other manufactured goods, for which there is much less evidence, arrived in Britain in large quantities, being shipped to major ports like London or York where, at both sites, quays are known. In return, Britain mostly exported raw materials such as metals, grain, leather and skins and wool, although there are indications of some manufactured goods being included. Occasionally more exotic articles arrived; a piece of silk damask is known from a Kentish burial, while different kinds of coloured marbles and other building stones from the Mediterranean were shipped from time to time to embellish both public and private buildings.

The increased opportunities for trade encouraged not only agricultural producers but also manufacturers. The materials known to Roman Britain remained the same as in the Iron Age, but the scale of working became much increased. It would seem that imperial control was maintained over the areas producing ores of lead and silver and these were for a time often worked under direct military supervision in Somerset, Derbyshire and Flintshire. But private contractors could obtain leases of the mines which were also possibly vested in the local authority. British lead certainly travelled to Gaul, while it is to be expected that much of the silver went to augment supplies to the imperial mints for coinage. Nevertheless some almost certainly reached the civilian markets and, as already noted above, there were silversmiths practising in several towns. Lead was extensively used for plumbing, for the manufacture of coffins and, alloyed with tin as pewter, for tableware. Tin itself was obtained from Cornwall, but little official interest seems to have been taken in it before the fourth century. Apart from pewter, tin was mainly used to give a silvery coating to bronze ornaments and vessels. Only one gold mine appears to have been worked in the Roman period at Dolocauthi in south-west Wales, and there again, as with silver, imperial control appears to have been exercised. These mines certainly seem to have been among the most efficiently worked in Britain with both open-cast and galleried versions in operation. Provision was made for their drainage by water-wheels and a number of aqueducts brought water to the site to aid both the mining and extraction processes. Again, however, some of the metal seems to have been sold on the open market and manufacturing goldsmiths worked there and in other places. Copper was chiefly obtained from north Wales, Anglesey and the Marches but not in sufficient quantities, seemingly, to warrant official interference. It was used, either by itself or alloyed as brass or bronze, for making many objects of personal adornment as well as tableware, statuettes, fittings on furniture and carts and military equipment. Indeed the objects occur so commonly in Britain that it must be doubtful if the local sources would have been sufficient to supply all the needs.

Iron was probably the most important metal to be produced and also the most abundantly occurring. Extensive extraction took place in the Weald, the Forest of Dean and in a wide belt following the Jurassic limestone from Oxfordshire to Lincolnshire. Its use was equally extensive and it became a necessity for the building industry as well as many other trades. Probably one of the principal advances in technology, when compared with the Iron Age, was the production of good-quality, well-tempered tools for carpenters, stonemasons and the like. Newly-introduced processes such as case-hardening and carburation enabled a mild steel to be produced which was of an undoubted advantage in the manufacture of tools and weapons of all kinds.

Of other industries, perhaps that devoted to the production of ceramic goods is the most fully documented. Wheel-made pottery was being made in Britain before the Roman conquest, but the quantities turned out after the invasion increased enormously. In addition to locally-produced wares, several major centres can be identified whose wares travelled more widely; among them in the first and second centuries can be quoted Colchester, Mancetter-Hartshill, the Isle of Purbeck, the Nene valley and Cantley, Doncaster, most of which manufactured their own characteristic vessels. A good deal of research has been done recently to show the distant markets which these areas often served in addition to their own localities. An extension of the industry produced both brick and tile, which were required in great quantities for building construction. Unlike the pottery industry, however, which remained very much in the hands of individual potters or small firms, most brick production seems to have been undertaken by larger concerns. The imperial procurator's department made bricks and tiles for use in public and official buildings in London, while the municipal authority at Gloucester likewise possessed its own kilns; in each case stamps on the products denoted ownership. Other large private firms are known in the Cirencester region. Moreover, the army frequently provided its own materials, sometimes amalgamating the production of brick and tile with pottery; works depots are thought to have existed outside most legionary fortresses, like that known at Holt, Denbighshire, which served the fortress at Chester.

There were certainly other industries connected with textiles and leather, but they are much less susceptible to archaeological investigation since most of the materials will have perished. One literary source does, however, mention an imperial weaving mill, probably at Winchester, but the building has never been identified. Occasionally water-logged conditions on a site will enable some evidence to survive, such as that which suggests a large tannery at Catterick, but they tend to be rare. Equally, the evidence for other extractive industries only rarely survives to indicate the stone, gravel, sand or clay quarries which provided the raw materials of the building industry, or for open-cast coal-mines, which yielded fuel for both industrial and domestic purposes; most have been destroyed in more recent workings. Salt, on the other hand, an essential requirement for curing skins, preserving meat and fish and as an element in the diet, was extracted from sea-water in numerous places round the coast, such as in the Thames and Severn estuaries and the Wash. A good deal of evidence has survived to show how the process worked first by the initial concentration, and then by the final evaporation, of sea-water in ceramic pans over open fires.

Another major benefit of the *pax Romana* was the establishment of an adequate system of law and order, administered at different levels. In most provinces native laws, where they existed, were still respected, but the Roman system of administration provided proper courts where disputes could be settled and arbitration obtained. Most minor cases could be tried by the local magistrates, but they were under an obligation to remit more important ones to the governor's assize court. Roman citizens had always to abide by Roman law, so that conflicts could, and did, arise between Roman and native, which had to be settled. It was always open, too, for a Roman citizen to appeal to the emperor's courts in Rome, providing he had the money to pay the cost of transporting and maintaining all the witnesses until the case came for trial. We know of some instances where this must have happened.

It was probably in the realms of religion and burial that the least effect was felt after the Roman occupation. Many native cults continued in use, respected alike by both Briton and Roman. Some classical cults became popular with the native population and in doing so often received a veneer of celticism, frequently becoming wholly identified with a native deity. Fundamentally, the religious and superstitious beliefs of both sides were too close for much friction to be generated, and it was only with the politically-biased cults such as Druidism or Christianity that the Romans interfered. Similarly the belief in an after-life regulated the burial practices of both classical and Celtic worlds, provision for it usually being made by the inclusion in the grave of personal possessions, relating to the person's wealth, and by a supply of food and drink. Both cremation and inhumation were practised according to the prevailing fashion of the time. Some of the more advanced Iron Age peoples had erected barrows over their graves, which could be either square or circular, and the counterpart in the Roman world is to be seen in the elaborate circular mausoleum, often built wholly in masonry, but sometimes containing an earthen core. The only wholly foreign habit which seems to have been introduced to Britain was the Roman practice of marking a grave by means of an upright standing stone, bearing on it an inscription describing the dead person and sometimes accompanied by a pictorial representation.

'Pax Romana'

By and large, therefore, it can be seen that the Britons benefited materially from the Roman conquest; on the spiritual side little was gained. It might be argued in terms of modern political jargon that they lost their freedom when they became subject to the Roman imperial power. But in order to accept such a hypothesis, we would first have to establish that they were free in the real, and not in the modern political, sense before the Romans arrived, and that would be extremely difficult, if not impossible, to do. Admittedly tribal leaders could make war on their neighbours, or exercise arbitrary justice over their peoples, or even sell them into slavery, but that hardly amounted to freedom for the subject peoples under them. The only real freedom was enjoyed by the leaders themselves, so that for the vast mass of the population the Roman occupation can have made little difference; for many life would have been equally grim in both periods.

## Chapter six

# The people of Roman Britain — the army and the administration

During the first and second centuries in Britain, the head of both military and civilian administrations was the governor, who was personally appointed by the emperor. Since Britain was an imperial as opposed to a senatorial province, and contained more than one legion, he was normally a man who had been consul in Rome but who, for reasons of protocol, took the lower title of *legatus augusti pro praetore*. Thereafter, with the division of Britain into two provinces in the early third century, Superior and Inferior, the government of Britannia Superior remained in the hands of a consul, while the lesser province, with only one legion, was governed by a man of praetorian rank.

We know the names and something of the careers of about three dozen consular governors, together with those of a half-dozen or so praetorian governors of Britannia Inferior. These men were drawn from the senatorial order at the top of society and, as with the lower orders, if entering public service, they followed a set career structure, the *cursus honorum*, which was carefully designed to provide a wide range of experiences, both civil and military, to fit them for their work. The first step taken as a young man was often a tribuneship in a legion, and at least one governor of Britain, Julius Agricola, so served his first appointment in this province. Tribunes acted primarily as staff officers to the legionary commander and would have been in an excellent position to gain first-hand experience in the arts of warfare and military administration. Then would have followed one of a series of lesser magistracies, after which the rank of quaestor would be attained, usually at the minimum age of 25, and at which stage entry to the senate could be gained; the duties of quaestor were mainly financial and the posts were distributed between the senatorial provinces, assisting the governors, and Rome, where attendance upon the emperor or consuls was required. Julius Agricola held the quaestorship in Asia, while Quintus Veranius and Neratius Marcellus, governors in Britain from *c*.AD 57–9 and 103 respectively, were both quaestors to the emperor. The post was the lowest of the regular magistracies, from which promotion, for a patrician, was often secured direct to the praetorship, or even omitted altogether, in which case he could proceed directly to the consulship; for a plebeian the normal step to the praetorship was by way of the office of tribune of the people. Originally in the Republic, the praetors, varying in number from time to time, were responsible for the administration of justice and also for certain military matters, but their importance declined under the principate and the job ultimately became an

48 Trajan's Column erected in the Forum of Trajan in Rome in AD 113 to celebrate the emperor's Dacian victories. The column carries a continuous spiral of decoration from top to bottom in which are shown scenes from the campaigns

honorary position. In the same way the office of tribune of
the people, while embracing much power in the Republic,
ostensibly in protecting the lives and property of the
common people, mainly from exploitation by the Senate,
likewise declined in importance, losing most of its practical
functions; nevertheless there was still political capital to be
made from the post, and most emperors personally
accepted its annual conferment. Among the British
governors, several, including Quintus Veranius, Julius
Agricola, and Platorius Nepos, builder of Hadrian's Wall,
are known to have held office as tribunes of the people
before proceeding to the praetorship. Ultimately in the
principate there were eighteen praetors and the minimum
age for attaining the post was set at 30.

The command of a legion would normally follow the
praetorship and at least two governors of Britain, Petillius
Cerealis and Julius Agricola, held legionary commands in
the province they were later to govern. Petillius Cerealis was
legate of Legio IX at the time of the Boudiccan rebellion, in
which the legion suffered a severe reverse, losing many
men. However, it does not seem to have affected his career,
for he returned to Britain as governor in the early 70s, when
Agricola was commanding Legio XX. The latter's experience of Britain was, therefore, further expanded by the
campaign into Brigantia, during which he would have been
able to assess the fighting qualities of the hill-people of the
north and so was, in many ways, better-equipped for
the war he was later to conduct there when he became
governor. After a legionary command, the next step was to
the governorship of a praetorian province, either imperial or
senatorial. Agricola became governor of Aquitania in south-
west Gaul; Platorius Nepos was promoted to be imperial
legate of Thrace, which only became a praetorian province
under Trajan. The term of office in such a post varied in
length but was on average about three years, after which the
person, if fortunate, might return to Rome to accept the
consulship.

Once a consulship had been held a whole series of senior
promotions came within reach, while often at this stage also
some form of priesthood was conferred, so uniting the
secular and sacred offices. Being a consular province, all
governors of Britain would have previously held a consulship, and in a number of cases came fresh from it to the
province. Such was the case with Petronius Turpilianus,
who succeeded Suetonius Paullinus in the aftermath of the
Boudiccan rebellion and who, together with his successor,
Trebellius Maximus, was largely responsible for the ultimate

pacification. Others went first to different provinces before
reaching Britain and Julius Severus, governor from
AD 127–33, served in Dacia Superior and Moesia Inferior,
on the Danube, before taking up his British post. But, even
though a man could become governor of an imperial
province immediately after his consulate, he had to wait ten
years before obtaining jurisdiction over a senatorial
province of consular rank. Consequently, most men who
were ultimately promoted to one of the two such senatorial
provinces, Asia and Africa, had seen much service elsewhere. Either of these two positions was considered the
crowning success of a career and a number of men who had
been governors of Britain, such as Didius Gallus, Vettius
Bolanus, Julius Frontinus and Lollius Urbicus, went on to
reach this peak of achievement, failing or after which, a
series of posts in Rome itself were available, perhaps including another consulship, or to be prefect of Rome, or one
of a number of positions supervising the most important
public works such as aqueducts or sewers, or one of several
religious offices. Julius Frontinus, for instance, not only held
a second consulship after leaving Asia, but also became
successively curator of the city's water supply and consul for
the third time. While in charge of the aqueducts, he completely reorganised their management on a much more
efficient basis, suppressing many of the corrupt practices
which had become associated with them. In so doing, he
recorded his activities in a treatise which is still invaluable in
considering the problems of urban water supplies in the
empire; he also found time to write books on military
strategy, much of which must have been based on his experiences as governor of Britain, when he was responsible
for the pacification of Wales. He also combined this work
with the sacrificial duties of augur. Lollius Urbicus became
prefect of Rome after being governor of Africa, which he also
combined with a priestly duty. Some governors of Britain
were not so fortunate. Both Ostorius Scapula and Quintus
Veranius died in office, while for Julius Agricola and for
some others it seems to have represented the virtual termination of their public careers. By way of contrast, Helvius
Pertinax, governor from AD 185–90, ultimately became
emperor for a few brief months at the end of the second
century, and another, Clodius Albinus, just afterwards, set
himself up as a claimant in the civil war of AD 193–6 and
was recognised as Caesar by Septimius Severus.

Such were the men, many of them among the ablest in the
empire, who were sent to govern Britain. Few, after the first
century, came from Italy, but were drawn from a wide range

of provinces. Julius Agricola was born in Forum Julii (Fréjus) in Gallia Narbonensis, Platorius Nepos came from Spain, Julius Severus from Aequum in Dalmatia, Lollius Urbicus from Numidia and Pompeius Falco probably from Cilicia in modern Turkey. Sometimes also, careers were helped to prosper by means of an advantageous marriage and it would appear that Petillius Cerealis was a son-in-law of Vespasian, while Agricola was undoubtedly aided by his marriage to a daughter of a Narbonensian senator. Such was the case with Rufinus; at the outset of his career in the equestrian order as a tribune of an auxiliary regiment stationed at High Rochester, he had married Julia Lucilla, a woman of senatorial rank, but he died while in north Britain; had he lived his wife would no doubt have helped his advancement to the senatorial order. It can be seen, also, that such men, before coming to Britain, obtained the widest possible experience of the affairs of state, both in civil and military matters. In time it became a regular feature for future governors of Britain to command a legion and hold office as a praetorian governor in one of the front line provinces such as Pannonia, Dacia or Germany where they might experience conditions similar to what could be expected in Britain. Some, nevertheless, were better administrators than generals, or vice versa, while others managed to combine the two roles without difficulty. The duties of a provincial governor might range from adjudicating in the courts between disputants claiming settlements according to both Roman and Celtic law, to the conducting of severe campaigns in the mountainous areas of Wales or the north, and it can be appreciated therefore that in the main these were no ordinary men; the career structure had seen to it that only the fittest survived. Admittedly, it is true that some provincial governors were also rogues, but Britain seems to have been spared the worst excesses.

In some provinces at certain times the military duties of a governor must have been paramount, in which case the civilian side of the administration could well have suffered neglect. Consequently, we find from the time of the Flavian emperors legal assistants being appointed to help in the courts. These men, also from the senatorial order, ranked as legates and were personally chosen by the emperor, the full title being *legatus iuridicus*; normally they were of praetorian status and acted as a deputy in legal matters, although the ultimate responsibility for all decisions remained with the governor. In addition such an officer might be called upon occasionally to act as governor, as happened in Britain to Antius Crescens early in the third century. We know the

**49** Dedication (*CIL* III, 9960) to Iavolenus Priscus, legal officer of Britain, from Nedinum (Dalmatia). The inscription reads:

*C(aio) Octavio Tidio Tossiano Iavoleno Prisco leg(ato) leg(ionis) IV Flav(ia) leg(ato) leg(ionis) III Aug(usta) iuridic(o) provinc(iae) Brittanniae leg(ato) consulari provinc(iae) Germ(aniae) superioris legato consulari provinc(iae) Syriae proconsuli provinc(iae) Africae pontifici P(ublius) Mutilius Publi filius Cla(udia) Crispinus t(estamento) p(oni) i(ussit) amico carissimo*

'To Caius Octavius Tidius Tossianus Iavolenus Priscus, legate of the Fourth Legion Flavia, legate of the Third Legion Augusta, law officer of the Province of Britain, consular governor of the Province of Upper Germany, consular governor of the Province of Syria, proconsul of the Province of Africa, priest of the sacred college; Publius Mutilius Crispinus, son of Publius of the Claudian tribe, ordered this to be set up under his will, to his dearest friend.'

names of five holders of the post in Britain, among whom should be mentioned the first two, Salvius Liberalis and Javolenus Priscus. Liberalis was acquainted with the younger Pliny, who regarded him highly as an advocate, and he came to the particular notice of Vespasian in a case involving a Greek millionaire. He was succeeded in Britain by Priscus, who was well known for his writings on Roman law and who later became head of a famous school of jurists in Rome. Both men served in Britain at the time of the great expansion of the province under the Flavian governors and it is likely that much of the successful political and administrative arrangements then made had been placed in their hands. Priscus, a native of Dalmatia, went on to follow a most distinguished career, governing in turn Upper Germany, Syria and Africa. Knowledge of the law and its operations, including advocacy, was therefore also an essential ingredient in the make-up of the senatorial career, it being expected that at some time or another a man might well have to plead on behalf of one of his clients. Under Hadrian, however, changes were made and a system was introduced whereby the senatorial jurist became supplanted by a professional lawyer from a lower social order, the equestrian class. In this respect it is worth noting one man, Volusius Maecianus, who began his career by commanding an infantry regiment under Hadrian. He then took to the law, rising to become prefect of Egypt, and was also chosen to give legal instruction to Marcus Aurelius before the latter became emperor.

The next most important man to the governor in the provincial administration was the imperial procurator, again nominated by the emperor, and entirely independent of the governor's jurisdiction. He controlled all financial matters such as tax and revenue collection and the administration of imperial estates and mines. Procurators were recruited from the equestrian order of society, the next in descent from the senatorial, and, as with that class, possessed their own career structure. To achieve equestrian rank it was necessary to be free-born and to possess wealth to the value of 400,000 sesterces as compared with one million sesterces for entry into the senatorial class. As a result the order was open to many provincials and even to retired legionary centurions. An *eques Romanus*, possibly called Macrinus, died at Colchester, where his fragmentary tombstone was found; he is the only British representative known, apart from imperial officials serving in the province.

Procurators occupied different levels of rank and their seniority was graded according to the the salary they received. The procurator of Britain commanded a salary of 200,000 sesterces which was on a par with most other provincial holders of the office. We have only the names of some ten or so in the British province and for most the position seems to have been the peak of their career, only a few thereafter rising higher in the imperial service. Perhaps the best known are Catus Decianus, whose actions stimulated the Boudiccan rebellion, and Julius Classicianus who was responsible for coping with the aftermath, and who died in office in London. His fragmentary tombstone unfortunately has missing that part which would have given his career in detail, but it tells us that he was married to Julia Pacata, daughter of Julius Indus, a citizen of Trier. Indus had distinguished himself in helping to crush a revolt in the Rhineland in AD 21, and had also commanded a cavalry regiment which, later, under its name the *ala Indiana*, was stationed at Cirencester sometime after the invasion. It is probable that Classicianus was himself a Rhinelander, and, being a provincial, might have been expected to show more sympathy to the Britons after the rebellion.

A recent discovery made at Inveresk, east of Edinburgh, which matches another inscription found at an earlier date, is an altar dedicated by another imperial procurator, Lucius Sabinianus. We can only speculate on the purpose of his journey to Scotland, which may have been connected with a census of the population for taxation, on one of the occasions when Scotland had been brought within the province, or with arrangements for the collection of customs duties on the new frontier.

The normal career structure of an equestrian embraced first a number of military commands, these being in succession the prefect of a quingenary auxiliary infantry regiment, tribune of a similar milliary unit, or in a legion, and prefect of a quingenary cavalry regiment. If a man was then singled out to command the larger, and rarer, cavalry regiment, one thousand strong, he was almost sure of further promotion. He might then be recruited into the procuratorial service, which, as already shown, contained many different levels, ending, as with Pompeius Homullus, the procurator of Britain early in Trajan's principate, by being procurator of Lugdunensis and Aquitania and culminating as the emperor's secretary to the treasury. Equally open to the equestrian order was the command of a fleet, and Maenius Agrippa had been prefect of the British fleet, with headquarters at Boulogne, before becoming procurator of the province under Antoninus Pius. An inscription mentioning another prefect of the same fleet shows how the equestrian order could be penetrated by retired centurions, for Flavius Quietus had previously been chief centurion of Legio XX, based at Chester, and while in this capacity he had led an expeditionary force to North Africa to help quell a revolt. Yet another way of being selected to command an auxiliary regiment as the first step to higher promotion was by entering the Praetorian Guard, the emperor's personal bodyguard. After sixteen years' service a man might be asked to undertake provincial service in a higher rank. So we find Paternius Maternus commanding an infantry regiment of Nervians, possibly at Netherby, Aurunceius

Army and administration

50 Altar dedicated (*RIB* 824) by M. Maenius Agrippa, tribune of the first cohort of Spaniards set up at Maryport (Cumbria):

*Iovi Op(timo) M(aximo) et num(ini) Aug(usti) M(arcus) Mae(nius) Agripp(a) tribunus pos(uit)*

'To Jupiter, best and greatest, and to the Deity of the Emperor, Marcus Maenius Agrippa, tribune, set this up.'

The full career of M. Maenius Agrippa is provided by another inscription which was set up in his honour in Camerinum (*CIL* XI, 5632). It records that he held command successively of the Second Flavian Cohort of Britons, the first part-mounted Cohort of Spaniards, the First *Ala* of heavy cavalry of Gauls and Pannonians, and the British fleet, ultimately becoming Imperial Procurator of Britain.

Felicessemus a tribune at nearby Bewcastle, and Flavius
Maximianus commanding an infantry regiment of Dacians
at Birdoswald; all had been seconded from the Praetorians.

Before collection of taxes could take place, detailed
surveys of property and possessions had to be made — a
census. Very occasionally a high senatorial official, or even
the emperor in person, supervised such work, but it was
more normally done, especially after the reform of the civil
service by Hadrian, by a procurator appointed for the purpose. Statilius Optatus carried out these duties both in
Britain and Gaul, while Gn. Munatius Aurelius Bassus held
the post of censor of Roman citizens in the *colonia* at
Colchester. The latter's career, noted on an inscription
erected in his home town of Nomentum in Italy, is characteristic; he held three auxiliary commands, two of which
were with the same regiment, the second cohort of
Asturians, stationed in Britain, before becoming procurator
and censor. He had also held various posts in the local
municipal administration of his home town, such as curator
of the roads, patron of the city, priest, aedile and duumvir.

Equestrian prefects or procurators were also employed to
govern certain imperial provinces, such as Rhaetia, in the
angle formed by the headwaters of the Rhine and Danube,
the provinces in the neighbourhood of the Alps, the two
Mauretanian provinces in north Africa and also Egypt,
although the latter is always considered as a special case.
Some provinces, such as Judaea and Thrace, were so
governed at first, but were later promoted to praetorian
or consular status. Unfortunately we know of only a few
officers who, having served in Britain, definitely reached
this peak of the equestrian career, although some authorities
consider that, for a time, after the division of Britain into two
provinces, Britannia Inferior was a procuratorial province
over which the consular governor of Superior exercised
control. If so, then both Oclatinius Adventus and Cocceius
Nigrinus may have held office in this position early in the
third century; both are attested on inscriptions, but there are
difficulties in accepting this interpretation.

We should also remember that equestrians, on accumu-
lating sufficient wealth, could be promoted into the senatorial order, especially in the later periods. Helvius Pertinax,
who, as already told, ultimately for a brief spell became
emperor, so began his career, starting as the prefect of a
part-mounted infantry regiment of Gauls, and then proceeding by the normal stages to provincial procurator, after
which he was elected to the senate and became in turn
governor of several provinces including Britain.

It will already have been perceived that there was a considerable overlap in the early empire between military and civilian appointments, with a high degree of interchangeability between them. In the provincial hierarchy, the legates of legions ranked high and could, theoretically, take charge of the administration in the absence of the governor, in the same way that we have seen could be done by a law officer. We have information on some dozen or more legionary legates in Britain, either from inscriptions referring directly, or obliquely, to them or from literary sources. One is known from an honorific dedication from Caerwent, the only example of such an inscription in Britain. Tiberius Claudius Paulinus commanded Legio II Augusta at Caerleon early in the third century. It is to be assumed that while there he performed some helpful act or made some gift to the Silures, whose *civitas* capital was at nearby Caerwent. In return, he may have been elected a patron, or more simply his act was commemorated by the erection of a statue and a record of his later career, made in the normal manner. He had also been governor of senatorial Gallia Narbonensis and imperial Gallia Lugdunensis, and, although it is not recorded on this inscription, he returned to Britain to become praetorian governor of the province of Inferior. There is an inscription from Vieux which confirms his British governorship, and one of his clients, Sennius Sollemnis, possibly returned with him as an assessor, working at the headquarters of Legio VI at York; this town was also the capital of Britannia Inferior, and the governor was, in addition, legate of the legion.

Another legionary legate who later distinguished himself was Vespasian, who commanded Legio II Augusta in the invasion forces. His biographer, Suetonius, mentions his vigorous campaign in southern Britain in some detail, and the damage inflicted by the legion on native fortifications and settlements has been attested by excavation. Vespasian was later given command of an army in Judaea to suppress a revolt of the Jews, and it was there that he became emperor, being so hailed first by troops in Moesia, during the civil war of AD 68–9. It is also of interest that in the same year the governor of Britain, Trebellius Maximus, was forced to flee owing to mutiny in the army. The civil war prevented the immediate dispatch of a replacement and for a short time Roscius Coelius, legate of Legio XX, acted as governor.

In the lower echelons of government service there were a large number of people, usually professional soldiers seconded for duty from army units and ranging from privates to senior centurions. Little is known of their careers or private lives, although tombstones, when found, usually indicate the office which they held at the time of death. Attached directly to the governor's staff were a number of clerks and orderlies who carried out duties in the *praetorium* (government offices). In charge was the *princeps,* usually a senior centurion; a tombstone from London, the provincial capital, illustrates such a man carrying both a centurion's vine-staff and a scroll. His name was Vivius Marcianus, married to Januaria Martina; he belonged to Legio II Augusta, and it has been suggested, not without reason, that he was serving in London as *princeps praetorii.* Tombstones of ordinary soldiers, as well as that of another centurion, representing both Legio VI and XX have also been discovered there and possibly represent men of detachments sent to London for ceremonial or guard duties, who were accommodated in a special fort built for them, in the first half of the second century, in the Cripplegate area of the city. Most interesting, however, is a fragmentary monument erected to the memory of Celsus, *speculator* of Legio II Augusta, by three of his colleagues. Thirty such officers were usually attached to the governor's staff and they were responsible for the arrest and custody of prisoners and also for executions. They are seldom to be found far away from the *praetorium,* and their presence in London is the most valid indicator that the town was the provincial capital and seat of the governor, at any rate from the late first century onwards.

Other government officials of junior status were stationed at various places in the province, mostly engaged in police duties, or in supervising the transport of army supplies. They were called variously *beneficiarii, regionarii,* or *stationarii* according to their work and were often attached to someone of superior rank. Hence, in Britain, there was a scatter of *beneficiarii* or *singulares consularis.* Three are known from Catterick, where there was an important posting station on one of the principal main roads to the northern frontier. One dedication, by a *singularis* Titus Irdas (?), to the god of roads and paths, would seem to suggest that he had some duty connected with highways. An apparent secondary inscription on the same altar mentions Varius Vitalis, a *beneficiarius,* who restored the stone, presumably to its original position. Yet another official of similar rank, whose name has not survived in full, set up a dedication there to the goddess Suria. It is clear, therefore, from the succession of men stationed at Catterick, that it was a supervisory centre for the provincial government. Further *beneficiarii* were posted at Winchester, Dorchester (Oxon.) and Wroxeter, in the civilian part of the province, while others occur with some frequency at northern forts. But apart from making general deductions it is difficult to say what their precise duties were at each place. A more unusual official, a *strator consularis*, Anicius Saturninus, was stationed at Irchester, near Wellingborough. He may have been in charge of stables which perhaps collected horses, on behalf of the governor, by way of taxes, or by direct buying, presumably as re-

**51** Drawing of an inscription (now lost), from Dorchester-on-Thames, on an altar (*RIB* 235) dedicated by a a *beneficiarius consularis*. It reads:

I(ovi) O(ptimo) M(aximo) et
N(u)minib(us) Aug(ustorum)
M(arcus) Var(ius) Severus
b(eneficiarius) co(n)s(ularis) aram
cum cancellis d(e) s(uo) p(osuit)

'To Jupiter, Best and Greatest, and to the Deities of the Emperors, Marcus Varius Severus, *beneficiarius* of the governor, set up this altar with its screens from his own funds.'

placements for the army, but the precise functions of these officers are not always certain. Another of similar rank, Cordius Candidus, appears to have been stationed at Dover, where he may well have been in charge, in the docks, of shipments crossing the Channel.

Regional supervision was usually in the hands of a centurion, and one is known from Bath. Severius Emeritus restored a shrine which had apparently been wrecked by vandals, which act he commemorated by the erection of another altar. Sometimes in special cases, also, supervision was combined with the command of an auxiliary regiment, as at Ribchester (Lancs.), where, towards the middle of the third century, a regiment of heavy cavalry of Sarmatian origin, from southern Russia, was stationed in the fort. At

**52** Part of a dedication to the Italian mother goddesses by a *strator consularis* at Dover. It reads:

*St(rator) co(n)s(ularis) Ol(us)*
*Cor[dius] Candid(us) [Mat]rib(us)*
*Italic[is] aedem [fe]cit v(otum)*
*s(olvens) [l(ibens) m(erito)]*

'Transport officer of the consular governor, Olus Cordius Candidus, built this shrine to the Mother Goddesses of Italy, willingly and deservedly fulfilling his vow.'

that time it was becoming increasingly common for troops to be recruited from outside the empire and, on retirement, for them to be settled in special areas around their forts. A documentary source refers to a veteran settlement at Ribchester, while two inscriptions from the site, together with a suggestion from a third, an exceedingly fragmentary altar, refer to legionary centurions commanding both the cavalry unit and the region, presumably containing the settlement. Aelius Antoninus was seconded for this duty from Legio VI at York; Floridius Natalis does not state which legion he belonged to, and in the third instance there is a reference to a centurion of Legio XX, based at Chester, whose name is missing.

In the procuratorial sphere of the administration, similar junior ranks existed, but we know little of them in Britain. There were probably fairly numerous assistants, who may have helped in the central office or have been given charge of an imperial estate to manage. That such men were often of lowly origin is demonstrated by an inscription from a building referred to as a *principia* at Combe Down, just outside Bath. It is a dedication to Caracalla in the early third century,

**53** Altar from Bath (*RIB* 152) erected by a regional centurion. It reads:

*Locum religiosum per insolentiam erutum virtuti et n(umini) Aug(usti) repurgatum reddidit G(aius) Severius Emeritus c(enturio) reg(ionarius)*

'This holy spot, wrecked by insolent hands and cleansed afresh, Gaius Severius Emeritus, centurion in charge of the region, has restored to the virtue and deity of the emperor.'

and mentions an assistant procurator, Naevius, who was a freed imperial slave and who was responsible for the building's restoration. Doubtless there were other men of his class elsewhere in Britain, for there must have been a number of imperial estates in the province.

Among professional soldiers the army obviously possessed its own promotional ladder, although as we have already seen, the higher officers had their careers linked with the civilian administration. The process says much for the high standards reached and maintained by what were, in effect, part-time officers. No professional, long-service army, of Roman or more recent vintage, has ever been happy under the command of young volunteer officers with restricted experience. Unless the officers can be respected for their ability and expertise in commanding men, much trouble can arise. In the Roman army this was to some extent circumvented by the existence of the centurionate, long-serving professionals to a man, which acted as a buffer between officers and men. Even today a young and inexperienced subaltern, if he is sensible, will gratefully accept help and advice, even on parade, from a veteran warrant officer or senior NCO, without in any way impairing the relationship between commissioned officer and other ranks: similarly in the Roman army, with one important exception. The young and green tribune in the first posting of his senatorial career ranked as the titular second-in-command of the legion. It can seldom if ever have happened in recent times that a newly-commissioned subaltern, even in the fiercest battle, would suddenly have found himself acting as divisional commander, after all his seniors had been killed; yet that could have been the equivalent position of the tribune. It seems unthinkable, therefore, that the tribune would have taken command in battle if the legate was killed. Nevertheless, tribunes were often given charge of legionary detachments working away from the base fortress, such as one who seems to have commanded a vexillation from Legio VI at Corbridge. Consequently, in the Roman army very great reliance was placed in the field on the centurions, one to each of the sixty centuries into which the legion was divided. For tactical, rather than administrative, convenience the centuries were grouped into ten cohorts, the first of which included in its strength most of the primarily non-combatant ranks. The centurions took their seniority from the number of their century and cohort, so that the centurion of the first century of the first cohort was the undisputed senior, professional, combatant soldier and would presumably have been *de facto* second-in-command in battle. It was therefore an extremely important position and usually held for only a limited time immediately before retirement.

We have already referred to an instance where a chief centurion had entered the equestrian order and been given command of the British fleet. Another post open to him on retirement was that of camp prefect of a legion. This officer was third in the hierarchy of the legionary command, but his

Army and administration

54 Dedication to the emperors Valerian and Gallienus (*RIB* 334) recording the restoration of the barracks of the seventh cohort of Legio II Augusta at Caerleon. The governor, the legionary commander and the camp prefect are all mentioned. It reads:

*Imp(eratores) Valerianus et Gallienus Aug(usti) et Valerianus nobilissimus Caes(ar) cohorti VII centurias a solo restituerunt per Desticiam Iubam v(irum) c(larissimum) legatum Aug(ustorum) pr(o) pr(aetore) et Vitulasium Laetinianum leg(atum) leg(ionis) II Aug(ustae) curante Domit(io) Potentino praef(ecto) leg(ionis) eiusdem*

'The emperors Valerian and Gallienus, Augusti and Valerian, most noble Caesar, restored from ground level barrack-blocks for the Seventh Cohort, through the agency of Desticius Iuba, of senatorial rank and the emperor's propraetorian legate, and of Vitulasius Laetinianus, legate of the Second Legion Augusta, under the charge of Domitius Potentinus, prefect of the said legion.'

duties lay primarily with the administration. Nevertheless, he could on occasion be left in command, as happened to the unfortunate Poenius Postumus of Legio II Augusta at the time of the Boudiccan rebellion. Ordered to bring the legion to Suetonius Paullinus' assistance, he failed to do so and committed suicide. We have evidence for some half dozen officers of this rank in Britain and from it we can see that they were often deputed to supervise intricate construction work. Domitius Potentinus of Legio II Augusta at Caerleon is recorded as having rebuilt the barrack blocks for the seventh cohort during the third century. Aurelius Alexander, sometime prefect of Legio XX at Chester and a native of Syria, perhaps retired to live in the civil settlement outside the fortress, for his tombstone records that he was 72 when he died. Another prefect of Legio XX had been chief centurion of Legio XXII Deiotariana before his promotion and had probably served in Egypt.

Our knowledge from Britain of the chief legionary centurions is equally slight. Some half-dozen are attested by inscriptions, mostly so fragmentary that the names are lost, while two are complete but anonymous. However, the reputed wealth of such men is demonstrated by an inscription from a cemetery area at Caerleon which tells of a chief centurion who paid for a funeral monument or burial plot, perhaps for a club, out of his own pocket. Another man, Cocceius Severus, attested in an inscription from north-west Italy, rose to become prefect of Legio X Gemina. He

**55** Fragmentary tombstone (*RIB* 509) from Chester of an un-named centurion successively of Legio V Macedonica, VIII Augusta, II Augusta and XX Valeria Victrix. It reads:

. . . ] *Pub(lilia tribu) c(enturio)
leg(ionum) V Macid(onicae) et VIII
Aug(ustae) et II Aug(ustae) et XX
V(aleriae) V(ictricis) vixit annis LXI
Aristio lib(ertus) h(eres) f(aciendum)
c(uravit)*

'. . . of the Publilian voting tribe, centurion of the Legions Fifth Macedonica, Eighth Augusta, Second Augusta and Twentieth Valeria Victrix, lived 61 years. His freedman and heir Aristio had this set up.'

had previously been chief centurion of the ill-starred Legio IX Hispana which was stationed at York until it was probably removed to Nijmegen in the early 120s. At about the same time, Pontius Sabinus, chief centurion of Legio III Augusta, stationed in Africa, was placed in command of reinforcements sent to Britain; the detachment was made up of 1,000 men each from Legio VII Gemina stationed in Spain, and VIII Augusta and XXII Primigenia in Germany. Later Sabinus entered the equestrian order, becoming a tribune in Legio VI Ferrata and subsequently imperial procurator of Gallia Narbonensis.

In contrast with the information on chief centurions, we know of over fifty legionary centurions who served in Britain. An analysis of the inscriptions serves well to emphasise the mobility and versatility of such officers, already indicated above, and perhaps best demonstrated by a fragmentary example, on which the name is missing, from Chester. This man had served successively with Legio V Macedonica and VIII Augusta, probably in Germany, after which he was transferred to Legio II Augusta at Caerleon, and finally finished up with Legio XX at Chester, where he died at the age of 61, probably while still in service. Indeed when the inscriptions are considered together, a very high proportion are found to represent centurions posted away from legionary headquarters, a considerable number of the dedications coming from auxiliary forts. In many cases, such as at the forts at Greta Bridge, Corbridge, Great Chesters, or in the quarries or on lengths of Hadrian's Wall, they were clearly in command of legionary detachments engaged in construction work. In others, they had been seconded or promoted to command auxiliary regiments, as may be suggested for a dedication to Jupiter at Bewcastle, where a centurion of Legio II Augusta is associated with a regiment of Dacians. A clear case of promotion is indicated by a similar dedication at Maryport on the Cumberland coast, in which Censorius Cornelianus, sometime centurion of Legio X Fretensis with service mainly in the eastern

56 Fragmentary dedication to the emperor Severus Alexander (*RIB* 1738), dated to AD 225, recording the restoration of a granary, in the auxiliary fort on Hadrian's Wall at Great Chesters, by a legionary centurion. It reads:

*Imp(erator) Caes(ar) M(arcus) Aur(elius) Severus Alexander P(ius) Fel(ix) Aug(ustus) horreum vetustate conlabsum mil(itibus) coh(ortis) II Asturum S̄(everianae) A(lexandrianae) a solo restituerunt provincia(m) regente [. . .] Maximo leg(ato) [Aug(usti) pr(o) pr(aetore) cur(ante)] Val(erio) Martia[le c(enturione) leg(ionis) . . . F]us[co II et Dextro co(n)s(ulibus)]*

'The emperor Caesar Marcus Aurelius Severus Alexander Pius Felix Augustus for the soldiers of the Second Cohort of Asturians, styled Alexander's, restored from ground level this granary fallen in through age, while the province was governed by . . . Maximus, emperor's propraetorian legate, under the charge of Valerius Martialis, centurion of the . . . Legion, in the consulship of Fuscus for the second time and Dexter.'

provinces, is shown as commander of an infantry unit of Spaniards. Other monuments reflect the reinforcements brought to Britain in the early third century. A tombstone at Piercebridge records the death of a centurion, . . . Gracilis, of Legio XXII Primigenia, who was almost certainly a member of the detachment, while two more altars from the same site record the dedications of another centurion, Julius Valentinus, also from Germania Superior, and of Lollius Venator, centurion of Legio II Augusta and commander of the whole force. Another sequence of inscriptions implies the posting of legionary units in forts away from their headquarters, such as the quartet of dedications from the exceptionally large fort at Newstead which record two different centurions of Legio XX who were stationed there with legionary detachments, together with an auxiliary regiment of cavalry, the Vocontii. A detachment of Legio II Augusta was stationed at Auchendavy on the Antonine Wall, since not only is the centurion in command, Cocceius Firmus, mentioned on four different altars, but also there is a build-

ing record, and two tombstones of legionaries, erected by
that legion.

Yet another aspect of Roman army life in Britain is contained in three altars from Bath, dedicated by centurions of
Legio II Augusta and VI respectively. These, together with a
further dedication by a standard-bearer of Legio II Augusta,
a tombstone of an armourer of Legio XX, and others of
private soldiers, have led to suggestions that Bath, with its
curative hot springs, was used as a convalescent station by
the army.

Certainly considerable care was taken of the soldier's fit-
ness, to the extent that even invalid diets were sometimes
prescribed for those in ill-health. Moreover, all fortresses
and most forts contained a hospital in which there would be
a number of wards and one or more operating theatres and
treatment rooms. The health of each unit was in the care of
professional medical attendants and orderlies, among
whom are to be found a number of Greeks, considered to be
the best medical practitioners of the day; two altars, each
inscribed with a Greek text, were set up at Chester by
doctors, Hermogenes and Antiochos. Normally such men
held the rank of centurion and there is a dedication from
Housesteads set up by Anicius Ingenuus, a medical officer
of this rank in infantry regiment of Tungrians, while
another, whose name is incomplete, was attached to a
cavalry unit at Binchester. We might also wonder at the
Greek dedication to Asclepius set up by Egnatius Pastor at
Maryport; Asclepius was a god of healing and therefore a
favourite deity of doctors. Nevertheless we should not be
too hasty in ascribing it to a doctor for, at Lanchester, the
tribune of a cohort, Flavius Titianus erected an altar also in
Greek to the same deity.

Medical attention by professional doctors was but one
aspect of the wide range of specialist services required by the
army. An armourer of Legio XX has already been mentioned at Bath, where his tombstone was erected by a guild
of armourers, but whether of Bath or Chester we cannot be
sure. A closely related post was that of the man entrusted
with keeping the arms store, one probably attached to each
century; Gemellus, carrying out this duty in a century commanded by Flavius Hilarius, died at Castlesteads, having
served most likely in an auxiliary regiment. Military
engineers are also known; Quintus was stationed at
Carrawburgh on Hadrian's Wall, but with which unit we
cannot be sure, while Amandus and Gamidiahus served at
Birrens. To these may be coupled, as having parallel duties,
Attonius Quintianus, a surveyor, who was posted to

Piercebridge. His work was connected principally with laying out the lines of fortifications and military buildings, while engineers, in addition to their construction work, might have been engaged on engines of war; surveyors might also have had to measure out land allotments. In a somewhat different category is a river pilot of Legio VI at York, Minucius Audens, who was probably employed in navigating supply vessels up and down the Humber.

57 Fragmentary altar (*JRS* lix, 235) erected by a Greek doctor at Chester. It reads:

ΠΑΝΥΠΕΙΡΟΧΑC
ΑΝΘΡΩΙΤΩΝ CΩΤΗΡΑC ΕΝ
ΑΘΑΝΑΤΟΙCΙΝ ΑCΚΛΗΠΙΟΝ
ΗΠΙΟΧΕΙΡΑ ΥΓΕΙΗΝ
ΠΑΝΑΚΕΙΑΝ ΕΙΗΤΡΟC
[Α]ΝΤΙ[Ο]ΧΟC[. . . .

'The doctor Antiochos [honoured] (the) saviours of men preeminent among the immortals, Asklepios of the healing hand, Hygeia (and) Panakeia.'

The efficiency of the Roman army depended on a cease-less round of drills and exercises, allied with first-rate records and logistic systems. Consequently drill-instructors were an essential part of the organisation; Flavius Blandinus held such a post and left a dedication at a temple at Lydney (Glos.). In legionary fortresses, covered drill-sheds were often provided for wet-weather instruction. Clerks of various grades are also attested; Celerinius Vitalis was a staff clerk of Legio IX at York. Another of similar rank, Peltrasius Maximus, who later served as a tribune at Bewcastle beyond

Hadrian's Wall, had been promoted by the praetorian governors, presumably for distinguished service in their office, while a third is known to have died at Great Chesters, also on Hadrian's Wall. The latter was probably attached to an auxiliary unit. Legionary clerks, occupying a more senior position than the foregoing, possibly being in charge of the record office, are known at both Chester and Caerleon, and another, belonging to an auxiliary infantry regiment, left a

**58** Bronze ansate plate (*RIB* 305) from the temple at Lydney (Glos.). The inscription reads:

> *D(eo) M(arti) Nodonti Fl(avius) Blandinus armatura v(otum) s(oluit) l(ibens) m(erito)*

'To the God Mars Nodons, Flavius Blandinus, drill-instructor, gladly and deservedly fulfilled his vow.'

Nodons was a Celtic god with attributes of healing, and was here equated with Mars, who in this context was often ascribed similar powers. Flavius Blandinus may well have been a drill-instructor attached to a nearby fort.

dedication at Ebchester. An accounts clerk, presumably serving in the pay office, was stationed at Corbridge.

The army also depended on a variety of brass wind instruments for signalling instructions in battle or in base camps. A trumpeter, Longinus, of an auxiliary regiment of Batavians, died at Carrawburgh; the instrument he used was long and straight. By contrast, the large curved horns which were employed on other occasions may have been used by a soldier of Legio II Augusta, Aelius Lucanus, who carved his name in one of the quarries providing building stone for Hadrian's Wall. There were also standard-bearers of different grades, depending on whether they belonged to legions, or infantry or cavalry units, whose positions demanded more than just the carrying of standards; they were normally responsible for the finances of their century and also had charge of the burial club funds, to which a soldier contributed during life in order to ensure for himself a decent burial with an appropriate monument. In addition there are some instances on the continent where standard-bearers appear to have been made responsible for extra-mural markets. The position was, therefore, comparatively senior and in many cases ensured promotion to centurion. Some dozen and a half men of this rank (*signifer*) are attested in Britain from both legionary and auxiliary units, such as Duccius Rufinus who was a standard- bearer of Legio IX at

York and who died at the early age of 28; or Flavinus, who
died at Corbridge, having been standard-bearer in the troop
of Candidus, of the cavalry regiment Petriana, the only
milliary cavalry unit known to have served in Britain; or the
nameless standard-bearer of an infantry regiment of
Batavians who died at Carrawburgh. Of another class
(*imaginifer*) there is Javolenus Saturnalis of Legio II Augusta
who had a dedication erected on his behalf at Bath, perhaps
in return for being cured of some sickness. It is an interesting
inscription, for it was put up by his freedman, Manius
Dionisias, and shows that soldiers even below the rank of
centurion could afford to purchase and maintain slaves.

There are many ordinary legionaries known from inscriptions and representing all the legions which served for
any time in Britain. Most, as might be expected, are connected with the main fortresses of the legions to which they
belonged, but there are a number attested from other places.
Three from Bath again indicate the possibility that the site
was an army convalescent centre, especially as two of them
died and were buried there. One in particular is worthy of
note, for it records the burial of Valerius Latinus, legionary
of Legio XX, who died at the age of 35 after twenty years'
service; if the figures are correct he must have enlisted at the
early age of 15. Apart from the special cases already cited
above there are also the tombstones of three legionary
soldiers from London, who were presumably in detachments seconded for duty in connection with the governor's
residence. From Lincoln, Caerleon and Chester come
examples which attest the mounted soldiers, usually
numbering 120 per legion, and which were normally distributed through the centuries. Individual inscriptions can
also indicate abnormal affairs, such as that of a nameless
*optio* (junior officer to a centurion), presumably of Legio XX
from Chester, who died in a shipwreck and whose body was
never recovered. On his tombstone the normal *H(ic) S(itus)
E(st)* (He is buried here) was reduced to *S(itus) E(st)* with a
space left for *H(ic)* to be inserted should the body have been
recovered. There are also scattered around the northern
forts a number of references to legionary soldiers; mostly
they would have been engaged on construction work, or
stationed as members of a maintenance party, or engaged in
works depots, such as the arsenal at Corbridge.

It can be appreciated from the foregoing remarks about
the Roman legions in Britain that a systematic study of all the
evidence can produce a comparatively fully-documented
account relating to several aspects. In the first place, the
movements of the legions, or of their detachments, can be

traced with considerable accuracy, even if, for the early years after the invasion, there are still a number of gaps for which the evidence is still lacking. We can see the legions fighting, or at work on peacetime activities. We can estimate their religious beliefs from their dedications erected to various deities, both corporately and individually. It is possible to make a rough calculation of the normal age of enlistment and length of service and also to obtain some

**59** Fragmentary tombstone (*RIB* 544), from Chester, of an *optio* lost at sea in a shipwreck, whose body was probably not recovered. It reads:

. . .] *opt*[*i*]*onis ad spem ordinis c*(*enturia*) *Lucili Ingenui qui naufragio perit s*(*itus*) *e*(*st*)

'. . . *optio*, of the century of Lucilius Ingenuus, and awaiting promotion to centurion, who died by shipwreck. He is buried.'

The missing H of the normal terminating phrase H(ic) S(itus) E(st) was never inserted

indication of life expectation, since a fair number died in service, but whether from accident, natural causes or in action we cannot say. From some tombstones we can learn of their families and, perhaps more important, their place of origin from which they enlisted. In the early days of the empire most legionary recruits came from northern Italy, but later many came from Spain and Gallia Narbonensis; all were areas where large numbers of legionary veterans had been settled in *coloniae*, from which the sons followed their fathers' calling. By the later second century, recruits were being drawn from a much wider area and the north African and eastern provinces, as also those nearer at hand on the

Rhine and Danube, were providing their quota for the legions serving in Britain. Occasionally also, tombstones carry valuable pictorial evidence of the dead person, which may well have been carved during his lifetime; such an instance is the memorial of the centurion of Legio XX from Colchester, Favonius Facilis, clean-shaven and in full uniform and as proud and arrogant a man as was ever pictured in stone. In contrast, there is the memorial to a cavalry trooper, Aurelius Lucius from Chester, which shows him bearded and moustached, and with longish hair brushed backwards. Cavalrymen were frequently depicted on horseback, with spear poised, riding down a fallen enemy, who is sometimes shown in a fighting attitude or else in a submissive, crouching position. The tombstone of a trooper, Rufus Sita, of a part-mounted regiment of Thracians from Gloucester is remarkable, not so much for the portrayal of the dead man, but for the craggy-featured barbarian lying beneath the horse's feet; in the circumstances of time and place the man is probably intended to represent a Silurian tribesman from south Wales.

Apart from the legions serving in Britain, there were as already indicated above a considerable number of auxiliary troops, both cavalry and infantry. We have already considered some of their officers, since command of an auxiliary regiment was an essential ingredient in the early career of the equestrian order. It is interesting to note, though, that the subordinate officers, such as infantry centurions or cavalry decurions, seldom gained promotion into the legions. The principal difference between legionaries and auxiliaries in the early empire lay in the former, but not the latter, being Roman citizens. Consequently, conditions of pay and service were better for legionaries, but when, in the early third century, citizenship was conferred on all freeborn inhabitants of the empire, these distinctions henceforward became less and less important, so leading in time almost to a complete reversal of roles. Unlike the legions also, the early auxiliaries were almost invariably recruited in the more distant provinces. Britain provided a number of regiments both of cavalry and infantry of different grades which served on the Rhine and Danube frontiers and in North Africa and Spain. A quick calculation shows that a minimum of some 17,000 men had to be recruited initially for these regiments over a period stretching through both first and second centuries. It should be noted that during this time units formed in one province were usually transferred to another for safety. Thereafter the regiment's strength was maintained in most cases by local recruitment, and we find a

Brigantian, Nectovelius, serving with the second cohort of
Thracians at Mumrills on the Antonine Wall, although there
is some evidence to show that territorial enlistment still continued with detachments from Britain. Undoubtedly, the
pride of the British regiments was the milliary cavalry unit
*Ala Flavia Augusta Britannica Civium Romanorum* which was
serving in the province of Pannonia Inferior during much of
the second century. Despite its name, which would suggest

**60** Tombstone (*RIB* 2142) of a
Brigantian, Nectovelius, who
served in an auxiliary regiment
at Mumrills on the Antonine
Wall. It reads:

*Dis M(anibus) Nectovelius f(ilius)
Vindicis an(norum) IXXX
stip(endiorum) VIIII nationis
Brigans militavit in coh(orte) II
Thr(acum)*

'To the spirits of the departed;
Nectovelius, son of Vindex, aged
29, of 9 years' service, of the
Brigantian tribe, he served in the
Second Cohort of Thracians.'

that its original formation took place under the Flavian
emperors, there is some reason to believe that it was the same
unit that Tacitus mentioned as having taken part in the civil
war of AD 69. Yet this seems doubtful since milliary *alae* were
virtually unknown in the Roman army before the Flavian
period. They always remained comparatively uncommon
units; no more than ten are attested and even one of these
was a camel corps for use in Arabia. The British regiment
was further distinguished by its grant of corporate citizenship, normally given to an auxiliary unit for some notable
service. If not so honoured during service, most soldiers
serving in these branches of the army were given the citizenship on discharge, which enabled them, among other
things, to legalize by marriage any association which had
been formed with a woman while they were serving. Enlist-
ing in these regiments was, therefore, an avenue to full
citizenship for many provincials. Conferment was made by
means of the diploma, inscribed on bronze sheets and

copied from the original document kept in Rome. A number of these records have been found in Britain, and give information on many of the auxiliary units stationed in the province as well as on their members. Although the number of regiments in Britain varied from time to time, at the maximum there were deployed probably some 90 cohorts and *alae* containing about 50,000 men, which far exceeded the legionary strength of the British garrison. Since many of these men would have settled in Britain on retirement, it can be seen that they represented a large potential reservoir of Roman citizens, so leading in time to a considerable increase in that element in the population of the province.

Considering the number of auxiliary regiments that served in Britain it is surprising that we, in fact, know less about their men than we do correspondingly for the legionaries. Records of some two dozen or so private soldiers have survived, together with about an equivalent number each of centurions and decurions. Mostly they belonged to the general run of *cohortes* and *alae*, but there are some individuals whose records represent more unusual circumstances, or detachments of a special character. At both Risingham beyond, and Great Chesters upon, Hadrian's Wall are attested special units of spearmen, originally recruited in the province of Raetia. At Risingham they had been placed under the command of the successive tribunes of the regular infantry regiment serving in the same fort and seem to have been present in the early third century. At Great Chesters the unit appears under the command of their own centurion, Tabellius Victor. A *decurio princeps* or chief decurion, Aurelius Armiger, probably of a part-mounted regiment, was stationed at Castlesteads. Three other *principes* are also mentioned on inscriptions from this site, Vic . . . Severus, Messius Opsequens and Aelius Martinus, but whether they were centurions or decurions is not specified. Moreover, the regiment stationed there seems to have been very conscious of minor distinctions and the order of precedence of its centuries, for the somewhat archaic terms *hastatus prior, hastatus posterior, princeps posterior* are all used on different building inscriptions; but they may refer to legionary detachments. Another interesting memorial of an auxiliary trooper comes from Malton (Yorks.). Aurelius Macrinus died there having served in the Imperial Household Cavalry in Rome, as a mounted bodyguard for the emperor. These men were normally selected from ordinary cavalry regiments, and it was customary for most to be recruited from the German and Pannonian provinces. Detachments of the Guard visited Britain from time to time when accompanying an emperor, such as those which came with Claudius, Hadrian and Septimus Severus. It may have happened that during one of these visits Macrinus liked what he saw of Britain and decided to retire there when the time came; perhaps he had been at York with Severus.

Below the level of the regular auxiliary regiments were a number of smaller units referred to as *numeri* or *cunei*. None were formed before the end of the first century, and the detachments were sometimes incorporated for specific functions or for the use of special weapons. Two units of lightermen (*barcarii*), one with the name Tigris appended, served at Lancaster and South Shields. It has been suggested that, in addition to their transport duties, they were expected to engage in offensive action during the late empire, for which their vessels would have been ideal in the shallow waters of the Lune estuary and Morecambe Bay, and in the mouth of the Tyne. A unit of Syrian archers, apparently, served at Kirkby Thore and can be matched by the regular cohort of Hamian archers, also from Syria, which served first at Carvoran, just behind Hadrian's Wall, and was then moved to Bar Hill on the Antonine Wall before finally returning to Carvoran. These Syrians belonged to one of the few regiments which retained recruiting links with its homeland. Another detachment, stationed at Burgh-by-Sands on Hadrian's Wall, had originally been raised among the Moorish tribes of north Africa. Other *numeri* were employed as long-range scouting parties called *exploratores,* and were stationed in the outpost forts beyond Hadrian's Wall; both Risingham and High Rochester possessed such men who seem to have been supernumerary to the regular garrisons. It has sometimes been suggested that they were not resident in the forts but lived in the native settlements in the surrounding countryside, which would have given them far better opportunities of obtaining information of impending attacks or movements of people. Certainly the forts concerned are hardly large enough to accommodate all the extra personnel, but they could have acted as headquarters, receiving information and relaying it to the appropriate authorities.

As with the legions, it can be seen that a parallel study of inscriptions and other sources yields information concerning the movement of auxiliary regiments and their soldiers. Examples have already been quoted to show how these units moved about the country; one further example will suffice. *Cohors I Baetasiorum civium Romanorum,* 500 strong, was originally recruited in Lower Germany in the area we now know as Holland. They first appear in Britain at Bar Hill

on the Antonine Wall, during its short second occupation.
From there they seem to have moved to Maryport on the
Cumberland coast, where they were commanded by the
prefect Attius Tutor. There then appears to have been a brief
return to the Antonine Wall, this time at Old Kilpatrick,
when they were commanded by Publicius Maternus but
were also associated with a centurion of Legio I Italica. This
legion was stationed in Lower Moesia and the presence of
one of its officers in Britain suggests legionary reinforcements, perhaps during the campaign of Ulpius Marcellus in
the early 180s. What happened to the cohort immediately
afterwards we cannot say, but by the middle of the third
century, if not before, it had been posted to the newly-built
Saxon Shore fort at Reculver, on the north Kent coast, where
it seems to have remained until the end.

The last section of the armed forces to be considered is the
Roman navy, which was in effect an extension of the army
and which, before the late third century, was mainly employed in the carriage of troops and supplies. There were
several fleets stationed round the empire, the two most
important being in Italy at Misenum and Ravenna. Fleets
were also stationed on some of the major rivers such as the
Rhine and Danube, while the Channel coasts of Britain and
Gaul were served by the *Classis Britannica*. Despite its name
its headquarters were at Boulogne, even though its commander was responsible to the British governor; in the
second century Dover, and possibly some other ports on the
south and east coasts, became closely linked with its activities. Its commander ranked as a prefect of the equestrian
order with equivalence to an imperial procurator. Aufidius
Pantera, who left a dedication to Neptune at Lympne,
became prefect under Hadrian after commanding a milliary
regiment of cavalry in Pannonia. Earlier, Baenius Blassianus
had been commander under Trajan. Maenius Agrippa is perhaps the most fully documented holder of the office; he
began his career as prefect of the second part-mounted
cohort of Britons in Moesia from where he was sent '*in
expeditionem Britannicam*' by Hadrian as tribune of the first
part-mounted cohort of Spaniards. He then took command
of the first *ala* of heavy cavalry of Gauls and Pannonians
before being promoted to the rank of imperial procurator,
which qualified him to be appointed prefect of the British
fleet. Finally he was transferred under Antoninus Pius to be
imperial procurator of Britain, having spent much of his
service in, or with soldiers recruited from, the province.
Another prefect, whose name is lost, had held not only the
command of the British fleet but also, at one time or another,

the imperial procuratorship of Lugdunensis and Aquitania,
Mauretania Tingitana, and Cappadocia and Armenia. From
the command of the British fleet he went on to be prefect
of the fleet at Ravenna, before apparently ending his career
as prefect of Egypt. Another, also nameless, apparently
held command of a combined fleet made up from Britain,
Germany and Moesia, was then praesidial procurator of the
Alpine province of Cottia, and also sub-prefect of the fleet at
Misenum.

But perhaps the best-known of the commanders was
Carausius, who, after a distinguished military career, had
been appointed prefect with special orders to suppress
piracy and raiding in the southern approaches of the North
Sea at the end of the third century. Suspicions reached the
authorities that he was diverting recovered goods to his own
use and orders were sent for his execution. Carausius, however, anticipated events and sailed for Britain where, with
the support of the army and the people, he set himself up as
emperor.

Of other officers, the Digest refers to a chief pilot, an
*archigubernes*, Seius Saturninus, over whose will there was a
legal dispute handled by the Flavian law officer of Britain,
Javolenus Priscus. From Boulogne there are some in-
scriptions mentioning ships' captains, *triararchs*, such as
Arrenius Verecundius and Graecius Tertinus; also a *bene-
ficiarius*, Lottius Secundus, perhaps attached to the prefect.
Tacitus refers to ships' pilots in his account of the mutiny of a
cohort of Usipi during Agricola's Scottish campaigns.
Detachments of the fleet also carried out repair work on
Hadrian's Wall, being responsible for restoring a granary at
Benwell and lengths of the curtain between Birdoswald and
Castlesteads.

Having considered the imperial administration and the
Roman armed forces, we can turn our attention to the part
played by British organisations in the administration at both
provincial and local levels. Unfortunately, there is a dearth
of relevant inscriptions from Britain and in many cases the
gaps have to be filled by reference to other, similarly-
governed provinces, such as those of Gaul or Germany. But
we must beware of applying such information too literally to
Britain, since Roman provincial administration was extremely flexible, and what suited one province admirably
may have been considered inappropriate for another.

At provincial level, the native population was represented
by a council, to which all constituent local administrations
sent delegates. It had very little power, although it did
possess the right of communicating directly with the em-

peror over the governor's head. It could also appoint patrons of the province, important men, well versed in affairs of state, who could, if need be, plead the cause of the Britons in Rome itself. Two patrons are known; Vettius Valens had previously occupied the post of *legatus iuridicus* in the province in the middle of the second century, and would have been an ideal choice. The other was Julius Asper who was a consul in the early third century, but nothing is

**61** The tombstone (*CIL* XIII, 3540) of a warship captain of the British fleet erected at Boulogne:

*D(is) M(anibus) Q(uinto) Arrenio Verecundo Tr(iarcho) Cl(assis) Br(itannicae) heredes p(onendum) c(uravit)*

'To the Gods of the underworld, and to Quintus Arrenius Verecundus, ship's captain of the British fleet. His heirs placed (this stone) in position according to his will.'

known of his British connections. Chiefly, however, the duties of the provincial council were concerned with the supervision of the Imperial Cult. They had to appoint annually a high priest who had to reside at the cult centre and organise the various festivals or demonstrations which the cult demanded; he also had to pay for them out of his own pocket, since the council was not empowered to raise money by means of taxes or levies. The first we hear of the cult and its servants is in the account of the Boudiccan rebellion by Tacitus, in which he recounts the complaints of the priests as they verged on bankruptcy with the excessive expenditure demanded. The cult centre then lay at Colchester, although there are slight grounds to believe that the provincial council later removed its offices to London, even though the principal temple remained at Colchester. Certainly in London the council was responsible for erecting a dedication to the deity of the emperor on behalf of the

135

province. Moreover, Claudia Martina, the young wife of a servant or slave of the council named Anencletus, died and was buried in London, but neither inscription provides absolute proof for the migration of the council.

At local government level, several different types of organisation existed. In the years after the invasion, use was made of client monarchs, rulers who were considered reliable by the Roman administration and who, by controlling tribal territories, would help to economise on Roman manpower. At least two such kingdoms are attested during the first century in Britain, with strong suspicions of a third, while later, others were used as confederates beyond the frontiers to help give stability in these regions. The southern Atrebates were one such kingdom within the province, ruled first by Verica and then by Cogidubnus. Verica is known from the coins which he issued and which circulated over parts of Sussex, Surrey and Hampshire. It has long been recognised that many of his coins owe much to Roman designs and even workmanship. Cogidubnus probably succeeded him in the early years after the conquest and reigned apparently until nearly AD 80. Although he issued no coins he is recorded on an inscription from Chichester and in a passage in Tacitus, who mentions that he had remained faithful to Rome 'down to our own time'. The inscription is normally interpreted to show that Cogidubnus held not only the title of client king, but also that of imperial legate. However, that part of the inscription is badly damaged and the reading has recently been disputed. Nevertheless, he seems to have been a man with considerable power and influence, even perhaps commanding detachments of Roman soldiers stationed at Chichester, and undertaking some duties which were normally reserved for the emperor, such as giving approval to the formation of trade guilds. On his death, however, his kingdom was divided into three *civitates*, the tradition of the kingdom being preserved in the name given to that at the centre, the Regni.

The other client kingdom for which there is indisputable evidence is that of the Iceni of Norfolk. They submitted to Claudius at the invasion and were allowed to retain their tribal institutions in a state, probably for a short time outside the province. Within six years, however, they seem to have been brought within it, after a minor rebellion had been put down by Roman auxiliaries. Their first ruler, known only from coins, was probably Antedios, but it is probable that he was deposed after the rebellion, when control passed to the more reliable Prasutagus. He, unlike Cogidubnus, appears to have been in no great haste to adopt Roman ways. Yet he was aware of the political demands of the Roman empire, even if he was not quite up-to-date, for he made Nero co-heir in his will to try to preserve his kingdom after his death. But it is doubtful if the share left to Nero was considered sufficient, the emperor at the time being greedy for cash. His widow, Boudicca, is well known from the accounts of the rebellion which bears her name, but the two daughters remain shadowy figures in the background. Perhaps he was unfortunate in having no sons. If indeed there were none, it is an interesting genetic commentary on the nature and character of Boudicca which fits well with our understanding of her.

Beyond the northern frontier in the 50s and 60s lay the kingdom of Brigantia, ruled by yet another queen, Cartimandua, whom we may suspect was also a client of the Roman state. She is known solely from references in Tacitus, and she appears to have been more of a liability than an asset, although for a time she helped stabilise the frontier district. Nevertheless, Roman arms had to go to her assistance more than once and, on the last occasion, they had to rescue her from the activities of her sometime consort, Venutius, who had declared war on Rome.

Outside the client kingdoms, at local government level, the organisation was split between the chartered towns — coloniae and municipia — and the native civitates, which were based mainly on the original Iron Age tribal structure. As far as can be judged, and the evidence is by no means conclusive even when that from other provinces is added, the civitates were administered in much the same way as the chartered towns, possessing a council of decurions and pairs of magistrates, the duoviri and the aediles. In some places quaestores also existed and had charge of financial affairs; whether Flavius Martius, who is described as a quaestor on a tombstone from Old Penrith, acted in this capacity for the civitas Carvetiorum, of which he was apparently a decurion, cannot be decided on the information given. He is the only possible local government quaestor attested in Britain. Decurions are scarcely better demonstrated. A nameless decurion of the colonia at Gloucester died at Bath at an advanced age; Volusia Faustina, wife of Aurelius Senecio, a decurion of Lincoln, died and was buried there. She was commemorated by a stone on which space was left for the later inclusion of a memorial to her husband; it was instead occupied by a reference to Claudius Catiotus, but under what circumstances we cannot say. Flavius Bellator, decurion of York, died aged 29 and therefore had become a councillor at an unduly early age, the normal qualification

137

being 30. He was buried originally in a stone sarcophagus, but when found it contained the body of a young woman who had usurped his place. At least one decurion of another province is also attested in Britain; Cornelius Peregrinus was tribune of a cohort serving at Maryport and also decurion of his home town, Saldae, a *colonia* in Mauretania Caesariensis.

No *duoviri* are known from Britain, although a fragmentary inscription, recently found at Cirencester, contains the letters VIR on what appears to be part of an imperial dedication. The word could be expanded to *duumvir* or *duoviri*, but could equally be *sevir*, a less important official charged with the local maintenance of the Imperial Cult. At nearby Gloucester, the initials, but no more, of some of the *duoviri* are recorded on the stamps placed on bricks and tiles from the municipal brickworks to denote public ownership. An aedile, Ulpius Januarius from Brough-on-Humber, is known from an inscription recording the gift and dedication of a new stage building for the theatre. He was a magistrate charged with the upkeep of public works in the *vicus Petuariensis*, the probable capital of the *civitas Parisorum* of east Yorkshire. There is slightly more evidence for the *seviri Augustales*, who, as already indicated, were the six officials in a local government organisation responsible for the Imperial Cult. They were normally rich freedmen and usually merchants, who were debarred from holding normal magistracies. Verecundius Diogenes and Aurelius Lunaris both held the office in York, while Lunaris was also a *sevir* of Lincoln. The former died and was buried in York, together with his wife, Julia Fortunata; Lunaris may have retired to Bordeaux, where he dedicated a fine altar, probably carried all the way from York, to the goddess Boudiga and on which his offices were noted. A very recent find from Lincoln records another holder of the office in the *colonia* on a dedication of a temple of the cult.

Evidence for the names of the urban sites and *civitates* is more prolific. Inscriptions refer to all four of the British *coloniae* and to London, while further evidence on them, and on other towns, is included in such literary sources as the Antonine Itinerary, Ptolemy's *Geography* and the *Notitia Dignitatum*. Two inscriptions, from Wroxeter and Caerwent, disclose respectively the functioning of the *civitas Cornoviorum* and the *civitas Silurum*, the latter also carrying a reference to the tribal council. Since most of the inhabitants were not Roman citizens, at least until the early third-century edict of Caracalla, all that was required of them, when it was necessary to state their origin, was the name of their tribe. Some thirty or so British inscriptions give this information which covers not only indigenous tribes but also some from other provinces. Doubtless many people remained all their lives in the places where they were born, but this small sample serves to show that there was, nevertheless, a considerable mobility among the peoples of the empire, Britain included, which was not restricted only to the army. For instance Similis of the Cantii is found dedicating to the Mother Goddesses at Colchester. Philus, of the Gaulish tribe of the Sequani, died and was buried at Cirencester. Tribeswomen of the Cornovii and the Dobunni are found respectively at Ilkley and Templeborough in Yorkshire. Verecundius Diogenes, mentioned above as a *sevir Augustalis* of York, came from the Bituriges Cubi of southwest Gaul, while his wife came from Sardinia. Regina, originally a slave of Catuvellaunian origin, was married to Barates from Palmyra in Syria and was buried at South Shields, while her husband appears to have died at Corbridge, after his wife's death. Detachments of Dumnonii, Durotriges and Brigantes all helped in the late fourth century to rebuild sections of Hadrian's Wall. Needless to say, Britons are also found in other provinces, usually as the result of enlistment in the army. A Dobunnian was serving in a British infantry regiment in Pannonia Superior. Ulpius Novanticus was born of a Coritanian father, Adcobrovatus, and enlisted in another regiment which served in Dacia; he received his citizenship on discharge and seems to have settled at Porolissum in that province.

There were minor levels of administration below that of *civitas*, each probably being divided into country districts or *pagi*. Some of these can be identified in Brigantian territory, but generally in Britain not much is known of them. *Vici* of varying types, the smallest units of built-up land, are also attested. The village settlements outside forts were so rated and were permitted a small degree of self-government under a pair of magistrates. In the *vicus* at Old Carlisle a loyal dedication made jointly to Jupiter and the emperor Gordianus was erected corporately by the villagers under their magistrates, towards the cost of which the inhabitants had personally contributed. Military *vici* of this type must have grown with surprising rapidity, for even during the short occupation of the Antonine Wall they sprang up outside the forts; the community of villagers at Carriden is commemorated in an altar to Jupiter. Other sites could also be legally classed as *vici*, including perhaps many of the civitas capitals; certainly Brough-on-Humber was one, as attested by the inscription of Ulpius Januarius. It is probable also that most minor towns and some major settlements of a

non-urban nature, would be given the title, such as Water
Newton, where the status is recorded on a pottery vessel
made there by the potter Cunoarus. Large towns could also
be divided into constituent *vici*. Lincoln is known to have
had two such divisions in the lower part of the town, named
after guilds set up in favour of the two deities Apollo and
Mercury.

It can be seen from this summary of evidence relating to
the army and the administration in Britain that a good deal
can be deduced about the people who were involved in it,
even if the record is patchy. It will be obvious, also, that the
quantity and quality declines in passing down the social
scale. This is, unfortunately, most true about the indigenous
inhabitants of Britain, a fact which will be best appreciated in
the next chapter. Nevertheless, it is sometimes surprising
how much information can be obtained even from the
slenderest sources, and without it our knowledge of Roman
Britain would be infinitely poorer.

# The people of Roman Britain — migrant and native

## Chapter seven

The principal difference between prehistoric and Roman Britain is the degree of anonymity which cloaks the former period. With the exception of some tribal rulers mentioned in classical literary sources or attested on coins, the people can only be studied *en bloc* as social or political groups. Only with the advent of Rome do the individual members of those societies begin to stand out from the crowd, and, when they do, we can often see them against the background of their activities. No one has yet calculated the number of named people who are known to have lived in or visited Britain in the Roman period, but if we include all those who denoted ownership of an object simply by scratching their names or initials upon it, there must be several thousand. They, therefore, provide a considerable reservoir of knowledge, which can often be extended to cover many of the social, religious and mercantile activities of the province.

As already indicated in the previous chapter, the Roman army was a considerable source of migrants to Britain, since the first units to arrive had all been recruited in other provinces. Many of the men, upon discharge, would have settled in Britain; it needed only a small percentage of that first army of some 50,000 men to provide the initial few thousand migrants, while the numbers would have gradually increased as regiments were exchanged, or others brought to reinforce the original garrison. The new *colonia* founded at Colchester in AD 49 is an admirable example of what was happening; it could well have contained up to 2,000 discharged legionary veterans, but unfortunately we know no personal details of the individuals who became its first inhabitants. The two centurions and one cavalryman whose tombstones have been found probably died at Colchester before the *colonia* was established and while it was still an army base. There is scarcely more information from the other military *coloniae* at Gloucester and Lincoln, although the latter has produced the tombstone of Julius Galenus, a native of Lyons and a veteran of Legio VI, but he cannot have been among the original colonists and presumably settled there later. Lincoln was also the place chosen for retirement by a nameless decurion of a cavalry regiment of

Asturians. Two other legionary veterans, Crescens and Aeresius Saenus of Legio VI, had, however, retired to the *colonia* at York, but this city was not a veteran foundation, having been promoted to colonial rank probably during the early third century. These are examples of retired soldiers wishing to stay near where they had served, presumably so as to remain close to their friends and companions. Similarly, we find that the civilian settlements around other

**62** Fragmentary tombstone (*RIB* 363) of a centenarian veteran of Legio II Augusta, from Caerleon. It reads:

[*D*(*is*) *M*(*anibus*)] *Iul*(*ius*) *Valens*
*vet*(*eranus*) *leg*(*ionis*) *II Aug*(*ustae*)
*vixit annis C Iul*(*ia*) *Secundina*
*coniunx et Iul*(*ius*) *Martinus filius*
*f*(*aciendum*) *c*(*uraverunt*)

'To the spirits of the departed. Julius Valens, veteran of the Second Legion Augusta, lived 100 years. Julia Secundina, his wife, and Julius Martinus, his son, had this set up.'

fortresses and forts attracted their quota of retired soldiers. Five examples can be cited from Caerleon: Flavius Natalis, Julius Decuminus, Julius Severus, Valerius Verecundius and Julius Valens, with the last three being specified as veterans of Legio II Augusta. The tombstone of Julius Valens also carries the information that he lived to the quite incredible age, for those times, of 100 and is, so far, the only centenarian attested from Roman Britain. The stone was set up by his son, Julius Martinus, and wife, Julia Secundina, who was herself commemorated on a separate memorial which recorded her age as 75. Similarly at Chester tombstones record some half-dozen veterans, including one from Legio II Adjutrix, despite its short stay in that fortress. Unfortunately they give little information beyond the man's name, rank and age, but we can note that Licinius Valens had originally enlisted from his home town of Arles in Gallia Narbonensis.

Although many auxiliary soldiers must also have retired

in Britain, there are few instances where the fact is actually recorded. Aurelius Tasulus, described as a veteran, erected an altar to the god, Belatucadrus, at Old Carlisle but he does not specify his regiment although it is more than likely that he served in the cavalry regiment stationed in the fort during the late second century; the *vicus* at Old Carlisle is one of the few in Britain whose corporate existence is indicated by an inscription. There was, of course, the known veteran settlement of Sarmatians at Ribchester, but apart from the three centurions in charge at one time or another, we know only of the wife, Aelia Matrona, the mother-in-law, Campania Dubitata, and the son, Marcus Julius Maximus, of Julius Maximus who was seconded from the Sarmatian cavalry to be a member of the governor's auxiliary bodyguard.

But soldiers were quite free to move around on retirement and it is likely that many did so, perhaps, if they had savings, setting up in business or trade and joining the already large band of migrant merchants who had come to Britain in search of wealth. Some of the latter have already been mentioned in the preceding chapter, such as Aurelius Lunaris and Verecundius Diogenes, *seviri Augustales* at York, with their connections with south-west France and possibly the wine trade; to them we can add a further inscription at Bordeaux recording another merchant trading to Britain, Solimarius Secundinus. Barates, from Palmyra, and husband of the Catuvellaunian woman Regina, may have been a maker of military standards. Philus the Sequanian

**63** A dedication from York recording the gift of an arch to a shrine by Lucius Viducius Placidus, who is almost certainly to be identified with the man of the same name who erected an altar at Colijnsplaat (Pl. 64 below):

> [I(ovi) O(ptimo) M(aximo)
> A(eterno) D(olicheno)] *et Genio Loci*
> [et n(uminibus) Au]g(ustorum)
> L(ucius) Viducius [L(uci) f(ilius)
> Pla]cidus domo [civit(ate)]
> Veliocas[s]ium [Pr(ovinciae)
> Lug(dunensis) N]egotiator
> [Brit(annicianus) A]rcum et Ianum
> [d(ono) d(edit) l(oco) d(ato)]
> d(ecreto) [d(ecurionum)]Grato et
> [Seleuco co(n)s(ulibus)]

'To Jupiter, Best, Greatest and Eternal, of Doliche, and to the Genius of the Place and to the Deities of the Emperors, Lucius Viducius Placidus, son of Lucius, of the country of the Veliocasses in Gallia Lugdunensis, merchant trading with Britain, gave this arch and vaulted passage as a gift, the site being given by decree of the councillors (of the city of York) in the consulship of Gratus and Seleuchus' (AD 221).

(I am grateful to Prof. J. E. Bogaers for his version of the restored text)

could have been attracted to Cirencester by trade. In addition a fair number of people who had trading connexions with Britain are known from continental sources. Among them we can number the pottery-merchant Viducius Placidus, native of the region around Rouen, who set up an arch at York and an altar at the mouth of the river East Scheldt in Holland; he was a rich man, for he was able to donate both the arch and part of a shrine, dedicated jointly

**64** Fragmentary altar from Colijnsplaat, the Netherlands, dedicated by a merchant trading with Britain. It reads:

*Deae Nehelenniae Placidus Viduci fil(ius) cives Veliocassinius negotiat(or) Britann(icianus) v(otum) s(oluit) l(ibens) m(erito)*

'To the goddess Nehelennia, Placidus, son of Viducus, citizen of the Veliocasses, merchant with Britain, willingly and deservedly paid his vow.'

to Jupiter Dolichenus, the spirits of the place and the deities of the emperors at York. It is not impossible that, like his two fellow-merchants at York, he was also a *sevir* of the colony. The sanctuaries to Nehalennia near Colijnsplaat, at the mouth of the East Scheldt, and at Domburg on the island of Walcheren, appear to have been very popular with merchants, and in view of their positions there must be a strong possibility that many of the people who dedicated there were connected with British trade, even though only a very small number made a specific mention of the fact. Among the altars recovered from the sites can be numbered those of the salt-fish merchants Exingius Agricola, a Treveran by birth but working from Cologne, Cornelius Superstis, Julius Januarius and Julius Florentinus, all of Cologne; the merchants of fish-sauce (*allecarius*) Secundius Similis, Carinius Gratus and Gatullinius Seggo; the pottery merchant, trading with Britain, Secundinius Silvanus; the freedman, Arisenius Marius, also trading with Britain;

and Commodus, a wine merchant. Two more, Vegisonius Marinus and Gimioga describe themselves as *nauta* which could mean either sailor or more likely in this context, shipper. Another, Julius Aprilis, was a veteran and some-time *beneficiarius consularis*, and may well have set up in business on retirement. At Cassel, a tombstone had been erected in memory of a Briton, Fufidius, who may have been a clothing merchant, while another, possibly from Britannia Superior, but who is nameless, seems to have been carrying on the same line of business at Marsal in Gallia Belgica. Xanten also has a record of a clothing importer, Priminius Ingennus, while Cologne has a general merchant, Aurelius Verus, again trading to Britain. Another probable trader in a slightly different category that we might include is Antonianus, who dedicated a shrine to the Mother Goddesses at Bowness-on-Solway. In three metrical lines he promised to gild the letters on the altar, if the goddesses caused his venture to prosper. It is more than likely that this refers to a trading expedition, either up the west coast of Scotland, or even across to Ireland. A scatter of Roman goods has been found on settlement sites in both areas, so there were doubtless trading connections across the frontiers to both parts.

Not only merchants travelled to Britain, but also crafts-men and professional people. A stonemason, Priscus, was working at Bath and set up a dedication to the local deity of the hot springs, Sulis; he came originally from the Chartres region of Gaul. In the pottery industry, the comparatively large number of Roman citizens who were involved, in the

65  Altar from Colijnsplaat, the Netherlands, dedicated to Nehalennia by a pottery merchant trading with Britain. The front panel (a) reads:

*Deae N[e]halenniae ob merces recte conservatas M(arcus) Secund(inius?) Silvanus negotiator cretariu[s] Britannicianu[s] v(otum) s(oluit) l(ibens) m(erito)*

'To the goddess Nehalennia on account of her good protection of Marcus Secund(inius?) Silvanus, pottery merchant with Britain, willingly and deservedly paid his vow';

(b) shows the rear face of the altar with simulated draperies; (c) shows the left-hand side and (d) the right-hand side of the stone

145

first century, with the manufacture of mortaria, can only imply migrant workers. From among them we might quote Attius Marinus who began at Colchester, before moving first to Radlett (Herts.) and then to Hartshill, near Nuneaton, which formed, together with the Mancetter area, one of the largest centres of the industry. Also working at Colchester were the five Sexti Valerii, possibly all freedmen and clients of a common patron, while two, and perhaps more,

**66** Fragmentary altar (*CIL* XIII, 8793) from Domburg, the Netherlands, recording a dedication to the goddess Nehelennia by Secundinius Silvanus, pottery merchant to Britain. The text is the same as Pl. 65 above.

Q. Valerii may have set up new workshops near Richborough. One of the latter, Valerius Veranius, had apparently moved from somewhere near Bavai and recorded the name of his new factory on some of his vessels as DOG(or C)AERIA FACTUM 'made at Dogaeria'; it is not, unfortunately, placeable. Even if his workshop had remained in Gaul, near the Channel coast, there must have been strong trading links with Britain, in view of the number of mortaria found in the province with the relevant stamps. Rutilius Ripanus was yet another, who set up in the same business at Radlett. A further group of potters came later to Britain, during the late second century, when attempts were made to found samian factories at a number of places, of which the most important was at Colchester. Since the production of samian ware requires special techniques as well as materials, it is likely that the potters had acquired the skills before coming to Britain. Most of the vessels produced here have affinities with East Gaulish types, which points to the probable origin of the people concerned. They did not restrict their activities solely to the manufacture of samian, but also produced colour-coated vessels and mortaria. It is

**67** Fragmentary altar (*RIB* 149), from Bath, dedicated by an immigrant stone mason from the Chartres area of France. It reads:

*Priscus Touti f(ilius) lapidariu[s] cives Car[nu]tenus Su[li] deae v(otum) [s(oluit) l(ibens) m(erito)]*

'Priscus, son of Toutius, a stone-mason, tribesman of the Carnutes, to the goddess Sulis willingly and deservedly fulfilled his vow.'

probably as well that they did so for the samian, owing to a lack of the right clay, was very poor in quality and never achieved much of a distribution or popularity; consequently the attempt was short-lived. There were perhaps some two dozen or so potters involved in the project, of whom the most prolific was probably Senilis. His stamped vessels are also found in East Gaul, including Rheinzabern, one of the principal factories for East Gaulish samian, and it is likely that his origin lay in that area.

Migrants were also interested in the extractive industries. The lead and silver mines of Britain were from the first exploited under government control as imperial estates. But private persons or partners, providing that they could

147

(a)

**68** Potter's marks: (a) graffito inscribed before firing on the rim of an Oxfordshire mortarium: *Tamesibugus*; (b) an illiterate potter's stamp on the rim of an Oxfordshire mortarium; (c) graffito inscribed before firing on a vessel made at Rushden (Northants), *Vitalis*; (d) stamp on a samian vessel manufactured at Colchester, *Senilis fe(cit)*; (e) fragment of imitation samian from Great Casterton, probably made nearby, it is stamped *An]andinus*

(b)

(c)

(d)

(e)

148

reassure the imperial procurator that they had sufficient working capital for the efficient running of the mines, could obtain concessions. Lack of the necessary funds was probably the reason why no obvious Britons appear in the lists in the early stages of development. Instead we find Roman citizens, probably rich freedmen, undertaking the work. Nipius Ascanius, whose name denotes an Italian origin, was engaged in the Somerset mines of the Mendips by AD 60 and later extended his operations to Flintshire. Claudius Triferna was also active in Somerset, and his interests later expanded to take in some of the Derbyshire mines of the Peak District. Another working in the same area was Julius Protus, whose pigs of lead were also marked, significantly, 'from the silver works'.

Among professional people we might mention Demetrius of Tarsus, a teacher of Greek and also presumably something of a geographer; he is mentioned by Plutarch as 'having just returned from Britain' where he had, among other things, been sent, probably by the governor Agricola, on an expedition round the north of Scotland. Two Greek inscriptions set up at York by a Demetrius, one a dedication to the deities of the governor's residence, the other to Ocean and Tethys, are almost certainly attributable to the same man. Unfortunately not all the references to migrants in Britain contain allusions to the nature of their business in the province. Some may well have been retired soldiers; others were possibly slaves or freedmen. The sources are often tantalising in their obscurity. For instance we may wonder in what circumstances a Dacian, Mettus, from the lower Danube region, came to be buried near Tetbury, some 20 km south-west of Cirencester. What was the business which brought Peregrinus to Bath from around Trier? He did not erect an altar to Sulis, the local deity, but to the gods of his homeland, Loucetius Mars and Nemetona, so it is unlikely that he came seeking a cure for a sickness. Why did a Caledonian, Lossio Veda, make a joint dedication to Mars Campesium and the emperor Severus Alexander at Colchester? A woman, Rusonia Aventina, from around Metz in Gaul, died at Bath and her tombstone was put up by a male heir; there was no mention of a husband. Was she, therefore, a camp-follower who came to Britain in the wake of the army in the days before soldiers could contract legal marriages? Or was she a freed slave? How can we account for Sacer, a Senonian from central Gaul, at Lincoln together with his wife and family? What was Valerius Theodorianus, a citizen of Nomentum near Rome, doing in York? He died aged 35, so he is unlikely to have seen military service, since

**69** Pigs of lead carrying the names of individual concessionaires or partnerships: (a) from Carmel (N. Wales), cast inscription *C(aius) Nipi(us) Ascani(us)*; (b) from Green Ore (Somerset), counterstamped on the side *Ti(berius) Cl(audius) Trif(erna)*; (c) from Syde (Glos.), counterstamped on the side *Soc(ietatis) Nov(aec)*; (d) from Hexgrave Park (Notts.), cast inscription *G(aius) Iul(ius) Protus Brit(annicum) (Sociorum) Lut(udarensium) ex argentariis*, 'British (lead) from the silver works of the Lutudarum company, (under the management of) Gaius Iulius Protus'; (e) from Churchover (Warwicks.), cast inscription *Socior(um) Lut(udarensium) Br(itannicum) ex argentariis*, 'British (lead) from the silver works of the Lutudarum company'

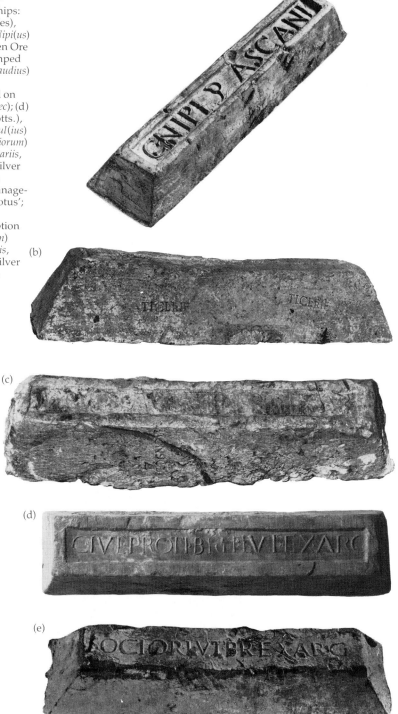

(a)

(b)

(c)

(d)

(e)

none is mentioned and the stone was erected on the orders of his mother. Was Hermes, a 16-year-old boy from Commagene in northern Syria, who was commemorated by a fulsome dedication in Greek at the fort of Brough-under-Stainmore, a slave of one of the officers of the garrison? Can we say the same about Labareus, a German, who dedicated at Maryport to an outlandish deity, presumably of his native land, called Setlocenia, or about the Raetian woman, Titullinia Pussitta, who died at Netherby, after she had probably been emancipated? What was the context in which another German, Lurius, erected a joint memorial at Chesters to his sister, wife and son? Was the Jewish boy, Salmanes, who died aged 15 at Auchendavy on the Antonine Wall, the son of an eastern trader who had chosen to cross the empire and do business on its most northerly frontier? Three Greeks are also attested in Britain, apart from those with medical connections already mentioned in the preceding chapter. One, Flavius Helius, lived in Lincoln with his wife; another, Antigonus Papias, who was probably a Christian, had migrated to Carlisle, while the third, Aufidius Olussa, died in London. Since most Greeks were exempted from recruitment into the army, it is probable that they also were merchants.

70 Tombstone (*RIB* 758) of a youth from Commagene (Syria) set up at Brough-under-Stainmore (Cumbria). It reads:

ἑκκαιδεχέτη τις ἰδὼν τύμβω(ι)
σκεφθέντ᾿ ὑπὸ μοίρης ῾Ερμῆ(ν)
Κομμαγηνὸν ἔπος φρασάτω
τόδ᾿ ὁδείτης· χαῖρε σύ, παῖ,
παρ᾿ ᾿εμοῦ, κ̄ηνπερ θνητὸν
βίο(ν) ᾿ερπη(ι)s, ὠκύτατ᾿ ἔπτης
γὰρ μερόπων ᾿επὶ Κιμμερίων
γῆ(ν). κοὐ ψεύσει, ἀγ[αθὸς]
γὰρ ὁ παῖς ῥέξεις δὲ σὺ
[καλόν]

'Let some traveller, on seeing Hermes of Commagene, aged sixteen years, sheltered in the tomb by fate, call out: I give you my greetings, young man, though mortal the path of life you slowly tread, for swiftly you have winged your way to the land of the Cimmerian folk. Nor will your words be false, for the lad is good, and you will do him a good service.'

151

**71** Tombstone (*RIB* 2812) of a young Semitic boy from Auchendavy on the Antonine Wall. It reads:

*D(is) M(anibus) Salmanes vixit an(nos) XV Salmanes posuit*

'To the spirits of the departed; Salmanes lived 15 years. Salmanes set this up.'

These cited instances of migrants among the population of the province must represent a very small sample of the total, especially as inscriptions of all types are rare finds in much of lowland Britain. If they are taken with those from other backgrounds, such as retired members of the army and administration, it would probably be not far from the truth to say that almost every other province of the empire was represented in Britain at one time or another. Not only is this a commentary on the freedom of the individual in the empire, but also it demonstrates that travel within it was comparatively easy and safe. Moreover, it indicates the way in which the British population would have become far more cosmopolitan over the years, so giving rise to the habitual use of several different languages or dialects and stressing the need for Latin to be learnt as a common tongue, if all were to understand each other.

Examination of the evidence also shows that many industries and trades of Roman Britain are represented by named practitioners of native descent; this is especially so in the hardware industries whose products more or less tend to survive burial in the ground. Nevertheless, care must be taken in assessing makers' names which are associated with portable objects, particularly of a personal nature, since they may have moved far from their places of manufacture, even perhaps being imports from other provinces.

A young slave, unfortunately nameless, was placed in charge of a goldsmith's shop at Norton in east Yorkshire, according to a building inscription which must have been built into its walls; consequently, we should assume that he was a practising goldsmith. Other workshops existed in London, Cirencester and Verulamium but we know nothing of their personnel. Similarly, with the manufacture of silver objects, a large factory has been identified at Silchester, although the workers again remain anonymous. There are, however, silver ingots of characteristic double-axe shape, which are found in late fourth-century contexts. It has been claimed that they were used for the payment of officials, in bullion rather than in coinage, which by then tended to change rapidly in value. These ingots were often stamped with the name of the factory and, although we cannot be absolutely certain that these were situated in Britain, we can be reasonably confident that it was so, because Britain remained one of the most important silver-producing provinces in the later empire. One ingot from London carries the stamp *ex offe Honorini*; it is possible, therefore, that Honorinus had a workshop in London. Two more are known from the Coleraine hoard of silver from northern

Ireland and were probably looted on a piratical expedition. One, broken in half, is stamped *Curmissi* (the works of Curmissus), the other *ex of Patrici* (the workshop of Patricius). The stamp of Curmissus is repeated more fully on an ingot from Kent.

But the extraction of silver was intimately connected with lead, since the ores are usually found in combination. Consequently we can assume that, in most cases where produc-

72 Fragmentary tombstone (*RIB* 955) of a Greek, from Carlisle. It reads:

*D(is) M(anibus) Fla(viu)s Antigon(u)s Papias civis Grecus vixit annos plus minus LX quem ad modum accomodatum fatis animam revocavit Septimia Do [. . . .*

'To the spirits of the departed and Flavius Antigonus Papias, a citizen of Greece; lived 60 years, more or less, and gave back to the Fates his soul lent for that extent of time. Septimia Do . . . (set this up).'

The formula used to describe his age is commonly employed in Christian contexts

73 Bone comb from London (*Britannia* ii, 299) stamped with the owner's, or maker's, name: DIGNVS

tion of lead is associated with individuals or partners, they may well have been engaged in the purification of silver. One example has already been quoted: that of Julius Protus in Derbyshire, where specific mention is made of the extraction of the silver content from the raw material. The same area also saw the development of a company of partners, of whom, incidentally, Julius Protus may have been one, called the *societas Lutudarensis*; Rubrius Abascantus was possibly

**74** Bronze statuette of a nude, but helmeted, Mars (*RIB* 274) from Torksey, near Lincoln. It was cast by a local coppersmith who donated the metal. The inscriptions read:

(a)
> (not shown) *Deo Mar(ti) et Nu(mini)b(us) Aug(ustorum) Colasuni Bruccius et Caratius de suo donarunt*

> 'To the god Mars and the Deities of the Emperors, the Colasuni, Bruccius and Caratius, presented this at their own expense'

(b)
> *ad sester(tios) n(ummos) c(entum) Celatus aerarius fecit et aeramenti lib(ram) donavit factam (denariis)* III

> 'at a cost of 100 sesterces; Celatus the coppersmith fashioned it and gave a pound of bronze at the cost of 3 denarii.'

another partner, for his name also appears on a pig of lead from the same source. A second group of partners worked in the Mendips in the late first century under the company title of *societas Novaec.*, but unfortunately they did not quote their individual names.

Lead was used extensively in Britain for plumbing, making coffins and other articles. One remarkable piece of work is the ornamented lead casket of late date from Caistor (Lincs.), made by an experienced plumber, Cunobarrus. It was made from lead sheet, 6.35 mm thick, on which the decoration and the maker's name were cast in low relief. He must have been proud of his work, for the name appears on all four sides. Two military plumbers may be indicated by the names Priuis and Aticurto scratched on a water-pipe from the legionary fortress at Chester. Lead was also alloyed with tin, normally obtained from Cornwall, to form pewter, which in the later empire was commonly used for making tableware. An ingot, stamped with the name Syagrius has been dredged from the Thames upstream from London, and may denote a manufacturer of pewter objects; judging from the distribution of moulds for making the vessels, it was not an uncommon occupation.

Copper and its alloys were widely used for a very large variety of objects, and coppersmiths were probably present in some numbers in most of the larger towns. Evidence for manufacturing smiths comes from Verulamium, Catterick and Colchester and a number are known by name from other sites as well. Cintusmus dedicated a bronze plaque to Silvanus Callirios at a temple outside the town of Colchester, while also from outside that town, came a large cake of raw metal, weighing nearly 10 kg, on which is stamped the initials *V.H. et B*, which probably allude to a partnership. Another coppersmith, Celatus, worked in Lincoln or nearby and was responsible for casting a small statue of a nude but helmeted Mars for Bruccius and Caratius, who paid him 100 sesterces; however, in return he donated a pound of metal, costing 3 denarii, free of charge. Hacheston, a settlement site in Suffolk, has produced a bronze scale-pan marked with the maker's name, Banna; interestingly, the name Banna is also recorded on another scale-pan from Sea Mills, near Bristol. Martlesham, not far from Hacheston, has produced a now broken statuette dedicated to Mars, made by Glaucus for Simplicia, while from Wereham in Norfolk has come a bronze steelyard stamped Advatucus. This seeming concentration of bronze-workers in East Anglia is a reminder that a small site at Wattisfield, not far from Thetford, has produced moulds for the manufacture of bronze razors,

**75** Bronze steelyard (*JRS* xlii, 105), from Wereham (Norfolk) stamped with the maker's name: ADVATVCVS

while brooches were made at Caistor-by-Norwich. A small bronze ansate plaque from Catterick, possibly attached originally to a military uniform, was stamped neatly in the centre with the name Dubnus. But all these small objects could easily have travelled far from their place of manu-facture. A very large number of bronze and copper vessels are stamped with the makers' names, but most, including such articles as paterae, jugs and flagons, were probably manufactured in other provinces and so cannot normally be taken as evidence for British coppersmiths. Although brooches occur with considerable regularity on Romano-British sites, many were imported from northern Gaul. There is, however, some evidence for their local manufac-ture and in addition to Caistor-by-Norwich, mentioned above, Baldock (Herts.) was perhaps also a factory. Few brooches indicate their maker, but one from the Maidstone area, of so-called 'Colchester' type, carries the moulded

**76** Bronze ansate plaque (*JRS* 1, 240), possibly a piece of a military uniform, from Catterick. It is stamped with the maker's name: DVBNVS

155

inscription *Nonn.F*, or *Nonnus fecit*. But we cannot be absolutely certain that Nonnus was working in Britain, although it is possible.

Blacksmiths must also have been ubiquitous, as well as the makers of more specialised iron-work such as cutlers or tool-makers. A fine, but somewhat weathered, tombstone of a smith, found at Dringhouses outside York, is unfortunately anonymous, but it depicts him wearing what may be

**77** Iron knife blade (*JRS* lix, 240) from Catterick stamped with the maker's name: VICTOR V.F

a leather apron over his tunic; he is forging with a hammer an object which he holds with tongs on an anvil. Many such men were extremely accomplished and an axe head, stamped L·G·R, from Newstead, was considered by the excavator to have been made by a professional tool-maker. He may well have been an army smith whose initial letters denote Roman citizenship. Another tool-maker, Martinus, is known from a chisel stamped with his name from London, while knives made by the cutlers Victor and Basilius have turned up at Catterick and London respectively, but perhaps only after travelling some distance from their place of manufacture. A maker of iron styli, possibly called Regnus, may also have had his workshop in London. Occasionally, the names of manufacturers of trinkets or toilet articles are recorded, such as the maker of bone combs, Dignus, from London.

Considering the quantity of pottery which was manufactured in Roman Britain, it is unfortunate that we know so little about the potters, for vessels were only exceptionally marked with the maker's name. The one class of vessel to be consistently so marked, at least during the first and second centuries, were the mortaria, shallow bowls probably used for macerating fruit and vegetables before cooking. Reference has already been made to some of the migrant potters who made these vessels in Britain during the years after the conquest, but it was not long before they were being turned out in some quantity by native manufacturers. One of the most prolific in the late first century was Albinus, whose vessels ranged in distribution as far as Scotland, but with by far the largest quantity occurring in the London-

Migrant and native

78 Iron knife blade from London, stamped with the maker's name: BASILIS

79 Iron awl from London possibly a leather-worker's tool, stamped with the maker's name: TITVI

Hertfordshire area. Some of his vessels are also stamped with the place of manufacture, which appears to be called Lugdunum, but which cannot be related to either of the Gaulish sites similarly named; it is most likely to lie between London and Verulamium, in an area which contained several known sites where mortaria were manufactured, such as Radlett and Brockley Hill. Indeed there are strong suspicions that Albinus had a son Matugenus, who was also a potter and who is known to have worked at the latter place. Another well-attested, but later, potter was Sarrius, who began his career at Hartshill near Nuneaton but later moved to Cantley, near Doncaster, presumably to be nearer his market which lay predominantly in the North.

Apart from mortaria, some other vessels were stamped, or otherwise occasionally marked with their maker's name. One such potter, whose stamp could be read as Indixivixus, was active in the Nene Valley, near Peterborough; he produced colour-coated imitations of samian vessels, mainly

80 Two chisels from London stamped with their makers' names: (a) MARTINI; (b) APRILIS F(ECIT)

(a)

(b)

derived from East Gaulish forms, together with other types. There were, also, a large number of semi-literate or illiterate potters who, in trying to follow the fashionable trend of stamping their products with their names, were often only able to create a die containing a variety of symbols. They are to be found most commonly in the Thames Valley area where in the fourth century a considerable industry was thriving. Of a number at least one potter, Paternus, was able

(a)

(b)

81 Stamped mortaria, both from Leicester: (a) *Albinus*. He was one of the most prolific manufacturers of mortaria in Britain during the later first century AD, operating apparently at a place called Lugdunum whose where-abouts has not yet been located, but which probably lies in the St Albans district of Hertfordshire. He appears to have had a son, *Matugenus*, who followed him in the same business; (b) *Sarrius*. Also a prolific producer, in the second century AD, who worked first in the Mancetter-Hartshill area before moving to Rossington Bridge, near Doncaster

to use an abbreviation of his full name, while some others coupled letters, such as SEO, with a series of symbols. The Thames Valley region also made some mortaria and one of the manufacturers rejoiced in the name of Tamesibugus. Exceptional circumstances occasionally provide further in-formation, and a potter, whose name is unfortunately in-complete, but which ends probably with the syllable -RICO, refers to himself in a graffito on a storage jar from Irchester, near Wellingborough, as being the son of another potter, and throws in the extra information that he had 'made the lower ones', presumably in the kiln. Another potter work-ing in the same area was Vitalis, while a graffito scratched on a pot before firing from a kiln-site in Kent recorded that Charmidanax had made 505 pots, which could have been a complete charge for a largish kiln.

If potters were somewhat frugal in naming their wares, tile- and brick-makers were not so unassuming. Moreover, the large flat articles which they were normally producing provided excellent surfaces for the employees to practise their writing skills either with exercises or by means of unofficial messages or comments. The brick and pottery industries tended to be rather differently organised, brick production being distributed probably between fewer but larger firms. Apart from official factories run by government departments, army units, or municipalities, to which refer-ence has already been made, a number of private firms are known from the stamps which they placed on their products. In many instances they were made up of three or occasionally four letters, which were the initial letters either of the factory or of the *tria nomina* of a Roman citizen proprietor. In Gloucestershire and Wiltshire two firms who used the stamps *Arveri* and *Juc . . . Digni . . .* are well known, while a third, equally prolific, used the initials TPF, sometimes followed by a fourth letter, to mark its products; from the same area there are also stamps such as LHS, LLH and VLA. In Buckinghamshire, there seems to have been a firm run by Arvienus, while in Surrey there was one run by

**82** Stamped tiles showing manufacturers' names or initials: (a) *Arveri*. The firm of the Arveri were active in the Gloucestershire/Wiltshire region as were also the firm which stamped their products; (b) *TPF* followed in this case by the letter *C*; (c) A tile stamped *RPGQQIVL FLORETCCRSM*: *R(ei) P(ublicae) G(levensium) q(uin) q(uennalibus) Iul(io) Floro et C(. . .) C(. . .) R(. . .) S(. . .) M(. . .)*. This tile was manufactured by the municipal brickworks at Gloucester when Iulius Florus and some other man, known only by his initials, jointly held the posts of *duoviri quinquennales*; (d) *LLH*, a tile stamp used by a firm whose products also circulated in the Gloucestershire region; (e) *SCM*, a tile stamp by a firm whose products circulated in the London region; (f) *PPBRLON*, tiles stamped with this legend *P(rocurator) P(rovinciae) Br(itanniae) Lon(dinii)*, were produced at an official brickworks near London run by the imperial procurator's men and presumably used for public buildings

(a)

(b)

(c)

(d)

(e)

(f)

Patendinius. At Wroxeter the letters LCH were similarly used, while Alcester has produced TCD and Farningham, in west Kent, CSE. Unofficial comments and remarks, which were usually scratched on the surfaces before firing, often relate directly to the workers in the factories; sometimes they are most revealing, others are quite obscure in their meaning. What, for instance, induced someone to record that Austalis, his fellow-worker, had been wandering about

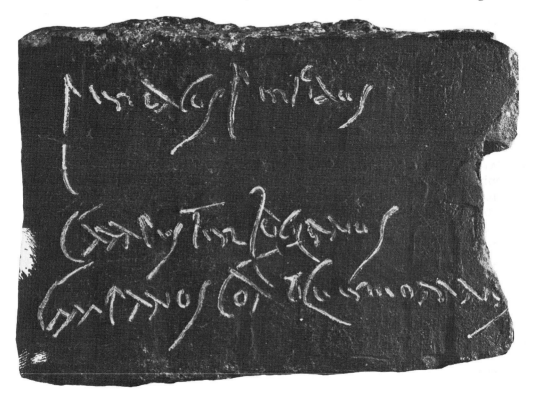

**83** Graffito on a tile from Silchester; it contains a list of names and terminates with the opening phrase from Virgil's *Aeneid* Book II:

*Pertacus perfidus* (untrustworthy)
*Campester, Lucilianus, Campanus,*
*conticuere omnes* (all fell silent)

on his own for the last fortnight? Was it really a writing lesson which caused a jumble of words to be scratched on a tile from Silchester, but ending surprisingly with the opening phrase, *conticuere omnes*, from the second book of the *Aeneid*, by Virgil? Did the tile-maker who scratched '*satis*' on one of his tiles really imply that he was fed-up, or was he simply recording the end of a production run with 'enough'? Straightforward comments are largely self-explanatory, as 'Candidus has made . . . roofing-tiles' from Cirencester; the anonymous reference on a box-flue tile from Dover that someone had made 550 of them; Cabriabanus from Plaxtol in Kent who was recording the individual manufacture of roller-stamped, voussoir-shaped, box-flue tiles; or Primus from Leicester who had made ten box-flue tiles. It has been argued that such workers would need to be taught Latin in order to record their production and other matters relating to the business, which might well be true. But we cannot allow brick-makers a monopoly of literacy and if it is true for them it is probably true also for all trades.

Although glassware and window glass were manufactured in Britain in several places, we have no definite records of its operatives, unlike many continental glassworks which often impressed their initials or names on mould-formed vessels. Many such vessels were imported to Britain and it is not impossible that some were made here, but no decisive evidence connecting them to a glassworks has yet been produced. Alcester has produced a glass bottle with the name of the factory of Sabellius moulded on the base; more normally the firm is indicated simply by initials, as with tiles.

Of the remaining extractive industries and their secondary workings, such as quarrying of various forms, that obtaining to stone can be best related to its workers. Millions of cubic metres of different types of building materials must have been excavated in the Roman period and there is a good deal of evidence for the quarries, especially in the neighbourhood of Hadrian's Wall. But there, as might be expected, and as mentioned in the preceding chapter, they were worked by the army, who left behind a large number of inscriptions cut in the rock faces, recording the names of units and personnel engaged. Other quarries are known in the vicinity of Cirencester, Bath, Canterbury and Lincoln and many other sites, but unfortunately civilian workers were less eager to record their activities. The migrant stone-mason at Bath has already been mentioned. In the same area worked the sculptor, Sulinus, son of Brucetus, who erected altars dedicated to the Suleviae at both Bath and Cirencester. Indeed, it has been claimed that the place where his altar was found in Cirencester was the site of his workshop, for it produced several other pieces of sculpture, which included the representation in relief of two triads of Mother Goddesses; alternatively it may have been a shrine dedicated to these deities. Not far away from a site near Stroud, a relief of Mars, in a gabled setting of reasonable quality, records that it was carved by Juventinus for Gulioepius. Another masons' or sculptors' workshop, unfortunately with no record of names, has been identified in the Lanchester, Chester-le-Street area of County Durham. It seems to have been working in the third century, mainly manufacturing altars, which travelled quite widely to such places as far apart as Old Carlisle and Wilderspool. The villa at Barnsley Park, near Cirencester, has produced a building stone with the name Firminius carved upon it; he may have been one of the masons employed on the construction. Two fragmentary names, . . .MAS and . . .AMUA, on a column segment from Fishbourne, might also indicate masons.

The clothing industry, both because its products were seldom marked and rapidly perish under normal conditions

**84** Altar (*RIB* 105) from Cirencester dedicated by a sculptor:

*Sule(v)is Sulinus Bruceti (filius) v(otum) s(oluit) l(ibens) m(erito)*

'To the Suleviae, Sulinus, son of Brucetus, willingly and deservedly fulfilled his vow.'

**85** Altar (*RIB* 151) from Bath dedicated by the same sculptor as in pl. 84 above:

*Sulevis Sulinus scul(p)tor Bruceti f(ilius) sacrum f(ecit) l(ibens) m(erito)*

'To the Suleviae, Sulinus sculptor, son of Brucetus, gladly and deservedly made this offering.'

of burial in Britain, is poorly represented. Woollen cloth must have been the commonest, although there is evidence for linen, and even silk, in the province; leather was used extensively, not only for boots and shoes, but also for garments. We have already introduced clothing merchants from the Rhineland, and it is perhaps worth mentioning that Britain enjoyed some distinction in the empire for its woollen goods. Two items of clothing, the *birrus Britannicus* and the *tapete Britannicum* are both mentioned in the price code of Diocletian, while a third, the *tossia Britannica*, is recorded on an inscription from north-west Gaul, in a list of presents sent by the governor of Britannia Inferior, Claudius Paulinus, to his friend and client, Sennius Sollemnis. Leather was frequently used for clothing both as under-

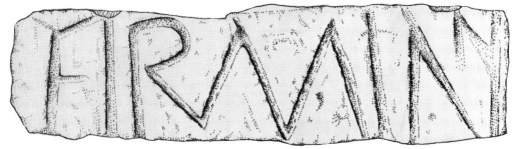

86 Mason's stone from the villa at Barnsley Park, near Cirencester. The name was probably FIRMINIVS

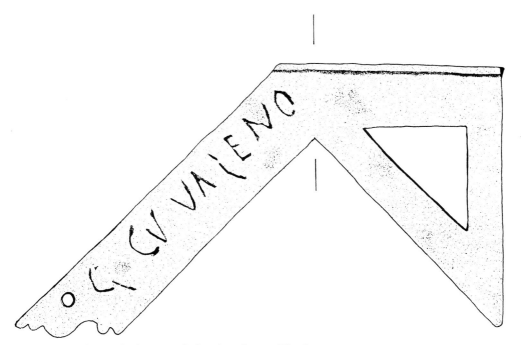

garments and top clothes, and also for shoes. The latter are occasionally stamped on the sole with the maker's name, and a lady's slipper from Chesterholm was marked by Aebutius Thales, a shoemaker of some distinction, judging from the quality of the article. Another small scrap of leather, possibly part of a garment or soft furnishing, and stamped with the name Verus, was found in London, and is

87 Mason's, or carpenter's, square of bronze, which belonged to Q(uintus) Cu(. . .) Valenus, from Canterbury

163

a reminder of the pair of leather bikini pants discovered there in a well.

In the woodworking trades, that of cooper is best represented; nevertheless we must remember that barrels travelled far and may, therefore, represent coopers working in other provinces. A number of internally-marked barrel staves have come from London and include the names, or their abbreviations: Fusc. Mac.; MCS; T. Senbon.; Aviti; and

88 Sole of a lady's slipper (*Britannia* iv, 332), stamped with the maker's name: *L(ucius) Aeb(utius) Thales T(iti) f(ilius)*, from Chesterholm (Vindolanda) near Hadrian's Wall

89 Fragment of leather from London, marked BVRDONIVS, who would have been either the maker or the owner

Galuisi; from Silchester we can add Verctissae and Nio. The staves were also frequently numbered in sequence, to ease the task of assembly. External markings, on the same barrels, probably indicate the name of the shipper or merchant; one of the London examples had been branded with the name Vettius Catullius, while two from Silchester were inscribed respectively with Sualinos and Herm., the latter probably an abbreviation for Hermogenes or some such name.

British merchants purveying food and drink are equally difficult to identify, although some may well be implied by the numerous graffiti which are carved or painted on pottery vessels. Among them can be numbered a considerable body of exporters to Britain of comestibles, like oil or fish-sauce, from Spain or Gaul. The amphorae or flagons used for transporting these goods are frequently stamped on the handles with the name of the factory from which the contents came. Alternatively they were marked on the body of the container by painting or scratching, such as those from Silchester carrying either the stamps of the Scimnian estate in southern Spain, or the name Junius Melissus, who appears to have been the estate's proprietor, or that from London which has painted on the neck: 'twin wine, produce of Aurelius, bailiff of Munatius Celer'.

Another class of merchant, with perhaps an ethical bias, is that which made up ointments for medicinal purposes. These were apparently made in cakes, either for direct application or for solution first in an appropriate liquid such as vinegar or wine; the cakes were stamped with the maker's name, the type of ointment and its purpose, the stamp being usually carved from a soft stone. At Kenchester, Aurelius Polychronidus was marketing salves made of gall, helio-

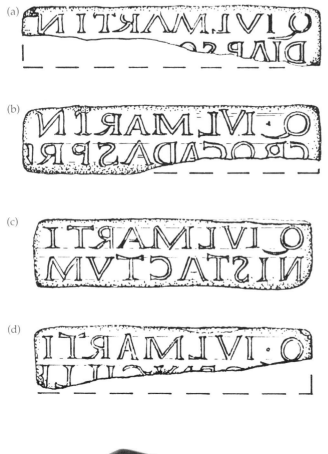

(a)

(b)

(c)

(d)

90 Drawing of the four sides of an oculist's ointment stamp from Chester (*Britannia* viii, 435). They read, respectively, in retrograde:

(a) *Q(uinti) Iul(ii) Martin(i). Diapso[ricum]*

'Quintus Julius Martinus, the anti-irritant.'

(b) *Q(uinti) Iul(ii) Martin(i). Croc(odes) ad Aspri(tudinem)*

'Quintus Julius Martinus, the saffron salve for soreness.'

(c) *Q(uinti) Iul(ii) Martini. Stactum*

'Quintus Julius Martinus, the unguent.'

(d) *Q(uinti) Iul(ii) Marti(ni). Pencilli*

'Quintus Julius Martinus, the ointments.'

91 A similar stamp (*JRS* liv, 181) to Pl. 90 above, from Kenchester (Hereford). The four sides read, again in retrograde:

(a) *Polychron(ides) dialepido(s)*

'Polychronides, the copper-oxide salve.'

(b) *Aur(eli) Polychronidi adyolithon post (impetum lippitudinis)*

'Aurelius Polychronides, the heliotrope salve after (the onset of ophthalmia).'

(c) *Polychroni(di) dia choles*

'Polychronides, the gall salve.'

The fourth side (not illustrated) refers to a swan-white salve for use at the onset of ophthalmia

(a)

(b)

(c)

trope, copper oxide and swan-white, while at Chester Julius Martinus was manufacturing an unguent, an anti-irritant compound, and a saffron salve for soreness. Another practitioner, Valerius Amandus, whose stamp was found at Sandy (Beds.) made vinegar lotion for running eyes, drops for dim sight, poppy ointment for use after inflammation of the eyes, and a mixture for clearing the sight. A very large number of the prescriptions were for application to the eyes, an indication that afflictions of this part of the anatomy were common even in Britain; dust and flies together can rapidly cause eye infections as can be seen in any underdeveloped country today.

Although nowadays men manufacturing such ointments would be accorded professional status as pharmacists, in Roman times they were probably considered as little more than merchants. But professional people did exist in Roman Britain, following much the same basic callings as today: law, teaching, priesthoods and, at its higher levels of practice, medicine. We know very little of the practitioners, but Juvenal mentions British jurists being trained to plead by Gauls. Lawyers must have been available to draft contracts such as those found on wooden writing-tablets in London. One, incomplete reads ' . . . this money when the applications have been drafted will be owed to me by Crescens or the party concerned; payment due on the Ides . . . first'. The second, even more damaged, refers to goods being sold, to the owner's shop, to ship-building and to permission being given for some action to be taken. Another carries an oath to Jupiter and the deity of the emperor, Domitian. A migrant teacher of Greek, Demetrius, has been mentioned above, and the large number of graffiti on walls, tiles and other oddments which appear to be writing exercises are a reminder that teachers of Latin were probably fairly numerous. Some priests and priestesses are also known by name. Calpurnius Receptus was a priest of Sulis in the important religious centre at Bath, where also the soothsayer, Marcius Memor, performed his duties. A priestess of Heracles (the Syrian equivalent of Hercules), Diodora, set up an altar at Corbridge to her deity, and it is likely that Pulcher, who set up a companion altar to Astarte, the consort of Heracles, was also a priest. Neither dedicator is a Roman citizen and both altars are inscribed in Greek. Another altar from the area of Hadrian's Wall refers to Apollonius, a priest of Nemesis, and one from near Milecastle 3 gives the name of Julius Maximus, but the name of the deity he served is missing. Medical practitioners have already been mentioned in military contexts, but none are known from purely civilian sources. However, a chance find made sometime ago in the Thames near Taplow has recently been newly interpreted, to give a reference to a specialist veterinary physician. Unfortunately the name is incomplete, but the inscription, in Greek, on the side of a ceramic vessel refers to a *mulomedicus*, or mule doctor.

Also well attested in Britain are the two large social classes of contemporary society, the slaves and freedmen. Several

**92** Amphora sherd from Carpow with an incised graffito, in Greek, reading:

ΠΡΑΣΙ[.

Wine flavoured with horehound (το πρασιον) was recommended for chest complaints in early medicine

**93** Graffito incised on a ceramic vessel found in the river Thames near Taplow (*Britannia* vii, 279). It had probably been used as a cinerary urn to contain the ashes of a mule doctor. The second, and only comprehensible line, reads, in Greek:

. . .]ΜΑΝΤΙΟΣΜΥΛΟΦΙΣΙ[. . .

. . .]Mantius mule-doctor [. . .

167

tombstones and some altars were set up by the latter, since normally a slave received his freedom on the death of his master. Two altars mentioning a legionary centurion, Aufidius Maximus, at Bath were set up by his freedmen, Aufidius Eutuches and Aufidius Lemnus, while a tombstone of a legionary standard-bearer, Iavolenus Saturnalis, was likewise erected by his freedman, Manius Dionisias, at the same town. Caecilius Musicus the freedman of Caecilius

**94** Tombstone (*RIB* 560) of three young slaves, dedicated by their master, from Chester. It reads:

*Dis Manibus Atil(i)an(us) e[t] Antiat[i]lianus an(norum) X Protus an(norum) XII Pompeius Optatus dominus f(aciendum) c(uravit)*

'To the spirits of the departed, Atilianus and Antiatilianus, aged 10, Protus, aged 12; their master, Pompeius Optatus, had this set up.'

Rufus, a decurion of York, is recorded as having dedicated the coffin of Rufus' wife, Aelia Severa. Sometimes also a master would erect a memorial to a slave or freedman, such as can be seen on two tombstones from Chester: Asurius Fortis put up a memorial to his freedman Etacontius, and Pompeius Optatus commemorated his three young slaves, the twins Atilianus and Antiatilianus, aged 10, and Protus, aged 12. Occasionally a freedman was also made the heir of his master, as was the case of Aristio who became heir to a nameless centurion at Chester. Another interesting document in this context is a wooden writing-tablet from London which is in the form of a letter from a master, Rufus, son of Callisunus, to his slave, Epillicus, who was probably acting as a bailiff or manager of a business. It contains an injunction to make a list and send it to his master, and also to look after everything carefully, ending finally with an instruction to sell a slave-girl. It is also apparent from a tombstone at

Halton Chesters that even slaves could form their own burial clubs, for a nameless slave of Hardalio was commemorated by his fellow-slaves. Several imperial freedmen certainly visited Britain and some may have settled. Publius Nikomedes dedicated to the goddess Britannia at York, while another reached Housesteads. A third, Aquilinus, dedicated an altar to Jupiter in London to commemorate the restoration of a temple, and must have been a comparatively rich man.

Needless to say there is a very large group of inscriptions from Britain which contain no references to occupations, but from them we can discern family groups, in which most types of relationship have been recorded, or we can make deductions about peoples' beliefs and superstitions. From the *vicus* outside the fort at Old Penrith, there is a tombstone set up by Limisius to the memory of his 45-year-old-wife, Aicetuos, and his 12-year-old daughter, Lattio. In the same place a legionary tribune, Claudius Severus, records the death of his 13-year-old adopted daughter, Ylas; another foster-child is mentioned on a fragmentary tombstone from York, while an 18-year-old girl, Mercatilla, is oddly described as freedwoman and adopted daughter of Magnius at Bath, the implication being that she was the daughter of a slave. York also possesses some excellent examples of family tombstones, such as that erected by Aeresius Saenus, a legionary veteran, for his wife, son and daughter. Only nine months separated the ages of the latter, who at the time of their death were both within the second year of life, while his wife was nearly 40. We might wonder what affliction carried them off apparently simultaneously. Also at York is

**95** Fragment of a wooden writing tablet from the Walbrook, London. The reverse side (not shown) sometimes had the address inscribed, in this case *LONDINIO*. The upper side originally had its recessed face filled with wax, into which the message was scratched with a pointed implement – a stylus. But the pressure applied was often sufficient to penetrate the surface of the underlying wood so that, although the wax has long since disappeared during burial, a faint trace of the message can be detected, but read only with difficulty. This particular letter reads in cursive script:

*Rufus callisuni salutem eppillico et omnibus contubernalibus certiores vos esse credo me recte valere si vos indicem fecistis rogo mittite omnia diligentur cura agas ut illam puellam ad nummum redigas. . . .*

'Rufus, son of Callisunus, greeting to Epillicus and all his fellows. I believe you know I am very well. If you have made the list, please send. Do you look after everything carefully. See that you turn that slave-girl into cash. . . .'

Rufus, probably a businessman, is obviously giving instructions to his bailiff or head slave about the running of his affairs during an absence. The letter is unfortunately broken at an interesting juncture, but the last phrase could be given the alternative translation of: 'See that you get your money's worth from that slave-girl'

169

the tombstone of Corellia Optata, the 13-year-old daughter of Corellius Fortis, who was sufficiently well-educated to compose five lines of Latin verse as her epitaph. From near York comes the inscribed sarcophagus by Valerius Vindicianus to his wife, Titia Pinta, and two sons, Valerius Adjutor and Varialus. From Silchester, there is a tombstone of the wife, Flavia Victorina, of a member probably of one of the most important families in the town, the Tammonii. A

**96** Fragmentary dedication from London (*Britannia* vii, 378) recording the restoration of a temple to Jupiter by an imperial freedman and his friends, or colleagues. It reads:

[*I(ovi) O(ptimo)*] *M(aximo)*
[*templum*] *vetus(t)ate conlabsum*
*Aquilinus Aug(usti) lib(ertus) et*
*Mercator et Audax et Graec(us)*
*restituer(unt)*

'To Jupiter best and greatest, this temple fallen down through age, Aquilinus imperial freedman and Mercator and Audax and Graecus restored to its former state.'

high proportion of such tombstones commemorate quite young children and are undoubtedly a reminder of the high rate of infant mortality, when quite common childhood diseases, in the absence of proper medical care, could often result in death. But it is also clear in many cases that, once the years of childhood had passed, there was a reasonable possibility of reaching quite advanced years. Actual ill-health is mentioned on a fragmentary tombstone from Risingham and refers to the substitution, for this reason, of a son, as heir, by another relative.

The religious dedications of Britain show a very wide spectrum of beliefs, embracing not only almost all the major classical deities and immortals, but also introductions to Britain from other provinces, as well as a considerable number of indigenous gods and goddesses; all indicate the functioning of the *interpretatio Romana*, whereby non-classical deities could be incorporated in the Roman pantheon. This fusion of beliefs is perhaps best demonstrated by the altar erected at Benwell, on Hadrian's Wall, to a purely local, Celtic deity, Antenociticus. It was put up by Tineius Longus, Roman citizen and prefect of the cavalry regiment of the Asturians, to celebrate his promotion into

**97** Tombstone (*RIB* 684) of a young girl from York. It reads:

[D(is)] M(anibus) Corellia Optata an(norum) XIII Secreti Manes qui regna Acherusia Ditis incolitis, quos parua petunt post lumina vite exiguus cinis et simulacrum corpo(r)is umbra insontis gnate genitor spe captus iniqua supremum hunc nate miserandus defleo finem Q(uintus) Core(llius) Fortis pat(er) f(aciendum) c(uravit)

'To the spirits of the departed: Corellia Optata aged 13. Ye mysterious spirits who dwell in Pluto's Acherusian realms, and whom the meagre ashes and the shade, empty semblance of the body, seek, following the brief light of life; sire of an innocent daughter, I, a pitiable victim of unfair hope, bewail her final end. Quintus Corellius Fortis, her father, had this set up.'

171

the highest social class of Rome, the senatorial order, and his designation as a quaestor.

The religion of the Roman state embraced first the Imperial Cult and the Capitoline Triad: Jupiter Optimus Maximus, Juno and Minerva. It is hardly surprising therefore that they became the chief official dedications of the army, both corporately and individually. There are nearly 150 dedications to Jupiter, in one guise or another, from Britain, the large majority having been set up at northern forts by army units or their personnel. A very large group of altars was discovered at Maryport on the Cumbrian coast. They had mostly been erected by the successive commanders on behalf of the units in garrison, and clearly indicate the practice whereby new altars were set up annually on the edge of the parade ground, while the old ones were buried nearby. Three different units are mentioned, and among the commanding officers was the tribune Maenius Agrippa who went on to command the British fleet and who later became procurator of the province. Another similar sequence of dedications to Jupiter, over twenty in number, comes from Birdoswald. All were erected over a period by the first Aelian cohort of Dacians, and thirteen different commanders can be detected. Altars or other forms of dedication to Juno and Minerva tend, however, to be less common. On the other hand dedications, either alone or in combination with one or more other deities, to the Imperial Cult were widespread over the whole province, showing that in time it had become an acceptable form of worship to native as well as Roman. The wording can take several different forms; the normal practice was to invoke the deified ancestors of the reigning emperor, as do most imperial dedications on both religious and secular buildings. A variant, however, employed the formula *Domus Divina*, to include all members of the imperial household, both living and dead, while a further alternative made use of the emperor's spiritual powers: the *numen Augusti*. A rarer form altogether, used solely by the army, were dedications to *Disciplinae Augusti*. One interesting series of imperial dedications appears in the north of Britain *c.* AD 213. They all with one accord protest in the most fulsome words the loyalty of respective units to the emperor Caracalla. It has been suggested that, after the assassination of Geta by his brother, some disaffection occurred in the ranks of the British garrison, which these inscriptions were intended to conceal.

In common with army and official practice, the cults of the principal classical deities are to be found in the higher centres of romanisation, such as London, the *coloniae* and some civitas capitals. Jupiter was accorded rights at Chichester and Cirencester, although in a form which was peculiar to the north-western provinces. At Aldborough he was linked with the Mother Goddesses. Minerva was linked with Neptune in a temple at Chichester which had been erected by the local guild of smiths, while in the great religious establishment at Bath she was combined with Sulis, the local deity of the hot springs; in the north she is equated with the tribal patron deity Brigantia. Mars was popular but more often than not in localised form where he was equated with a local deity and often took different attributes from those of the purely classical concept. At Lydney he was linked with the Celtic god Nodens, who was associated with healing, while in a shrine just outside Lincoln the dedication was to Mars Rigonemetos — king of the groves. Mercury was also fairly popular and seems to have been one of the deities associated with the chief religious centre of the Trinovantes at Gosbecks, near Colchester, but again there is more often than not a connection with a Celtic deity. Among other classical figures represented in Britain can be noted Apollo, sometimes linked with Maponus, as occurred near Carlisle, Diana, Hercules, Silvanus and Vulcan, together with Fortune and Victory.

Celtic deities were far more numerous, often possessing only quite localised attraction, and they tended to represent natural processes, places or powers. One of the most popular associations was with water and the shrine of Coventina outside the fort at Carrawburgh was built round a spring, into which many small offerings had been thrown over a long period of time. Another was the cult of the Mother Goddesses, practised widely over Celtic Europe, whose counterpart in the classical world was Ceres. It was basically a fertility cult connected with crops and regeneration, and usually the deities appear as a triple manifestation to denote their power. They, and a minor variant, were well liked in and around Cirencester, where dedications to the Sulevian Mothers and pictorial representations on stone were made. At York, the altar of the river pilot, Minucius Audens, was set up to the *Matres* of Africa, Italy and Gaul; at Benwell and Cramond occur the *Matres Campestres* — of the parade-ground — while at Binchester there were the *Matres Ollototae*. The latter derivative seems to have been popular with *beneficiarii*, for no less than two of the three altars so dedicated there were set up by these officers.

Some of the Celtic deities propitiated in Britain were

undoubtedly brought in from other parts of the empire, such as Gaul, Germany and the Danube area. Mars Lenus or Ocelus, known at Chedworth, Caerwent and Carlisle, originated in the Treveran area of the Rhineland, and Mars Rigisamus, with a representative in Somerset, had travelled from Aquitania. The *numerus Hnaudifridus* at Housesteads united a dedication to the deity of the emperor with three goddesses from their homeland, Alaisiagae, Baudihillia and

**98** Dedication in verse to the Syrian Goddess, from Carvoran (*RIB* 1791). It reads:

*Imminet Leoni Virgo caelesti situ/ spicifera iusti inventrix urbium conditrix/et quis muneribus nosse contigit deos:/ergo eadem mater divum Pax Virtus Ceres/dea Syria lance vitam et iura pensitans/in caelo visum Syria sidus edidit/Libyae colendum: inde cuncti didicimus./ita intellexit numine inductus tuo/ Marcus Caecilius Donatianus militans/tribunus in praefecto dono principis.*

'The Virgin in her heavenly place rides upon the Lion; bearer of corn, inventor of law, founder of cities, by whose gifts it is man's good lot to know the gods: therefore she is the Mother of the gods, Peace, Virtue, Ceres, the Syrian Goddess, weighing life and laws in her balance. Syria has sent the constellation seen in the heavens to Libya to be worshipped: thence have we all learned. Thus has understood, led by thy godhead, Marcus Caecilius Donatianus, serving as tribune in the post of prefect by the emperor's gift.'

Friagabis, while a detachment of the Suebian tribe stationed at Lanchester brought with them their own deity, Garmangabis. Another more popular deity supposedly originating in Germany was Vitiris, who seems to have appealed to a wide range of people. Carvoran has a group of altars so dedicated, and no less than three were put up by

Necalames, in each case, presumably, in return for favours received from the deity.

If German units brought their own gods with them, it is not surprising that we also find deities representative of regiments from other parts of the empire. The cohort of Hamian Archers from Syria, also stationed at Carvoran, naturally erected altars to their native deities and the Syrian Goddess and the goddess Hammia were commemorated not only on altars but also on a plaque, inscribed with ten iambic senarii, in which Syria was coupled with Ceres. There is also an altar to Jupiter Heliopolitanus, a derivative from the temple of Jupiter at Baalbek in the same province. Other eastern cults reached Britain at the hands of soldiers or merchants, giving rise to shrines or temples devoted to Serapis, Isis, Astarte and Mithras, in addition to another variant of Jupiter worship, again originating in Syria and given the name Jupiter Dolichenus after its place of origin. Among eastern cults mention should also be made of Christianity, which after AD 313 became a permitted religion. Before that date, however, it is naturally unusual to find any overt references to it, since they might have invited persecution, but there is evidence in literary sources for its practice in Britain during the third century, to which date probably also belong the Manchester and Cirencester acrostics, with their concealed Christian meaning.

In all this multitude of private religious dedications, we seldom receive any indication as to the reason why they were made, beyond the most frugal reference that so-and-so had fulfilled a vow made to the deity. What lay concealed, for instance, behind the erection of an altar at High Rochester to Silvanus Pantheus, god of woodlands and uncultivated lands, with a somewhat uncertain reputation, on behalf of the welfare of the tribune Rufinus and his wife Lucilla, jointly by his freedman Eutyches and his dependants? If we are to believe the evidence, not a great deal of good came from the act, since a fragmentary tombstone of a nameless tribune of the first cohort of Vardulli, set up by his wife, Julia Lucilla, may well have commemorated the same Rufinus; Julia Lucilla is described as belonging to the senatorial order, so that her husband, having made a good marriage, was cut short at the outset of a very promising career.

There is, however, a class of inscription which is usually a little more explicit. From time to time people scratched on a lead sheet a curse against someone who had wronged them, and either nailed it to a post in the precinct of a temple, or dropped it into a spring, so as to call down the wrath of a particular deity upon the head of the malefactor. Recent excavations made on a temple site at Uley (Glos.) have yielded over a hundred such curses. Another, found in association with a religious site at Ratcliffe-on-Soar (Notts.), invokes the help of Jupiter to recover a sum of money stolen from a man whose name was probably Canius Dignus. The god is invited to plague the thief with all sorts of uncomfortable pains, psychological and physical, and in return for

**99** Altar (*RIB* 1271) dedicated by the freedman of the tribune of an auxiliary regiment stationed at High Rochester. It reads:

*Silvano [Pa]ntheo [p]ro sa[lute*
*Ru]fin[i] trib(uni) et [L]ucillae eius*
*Eutychus lib(ertus) c(um) s(uis)*
*v(otum) s(oluit) l(ibens) m(erito)*

'To Silvanus Pantheus for the welfare of Rufinus, the tribune, and Lucilla, his (wife), Eutychus, the freedman, with his dependants, willingly and deservedly fulfilled his vow.'

Rufinus' tombstone is also known from High Rochester, although his name is missing (*RIB* 1288):

*. . . coh(ortis) I Vardul(lorum)*
*[. . . praef(ecto)] coh(ortis) I*
*Aug(ustae) Lusitanor(um) item*
*coh(ortis) I Breucor(um)*
*subcur(atori) viae Flaminiae et*
*aliment(orum) subcur(atori) operi*
*publ(icorum) Iulia Lucilla*
*c(larissima) f(emina) marito b(ene)*
*m(erenti) vix(it) an(nos) XLVIII*
*m(enses) VI d(ies) XXV*

'. . . to . . . of the first cohort of the Vardulli . . . prefect of the first cohort Augusta of Lusitanians, also of the first cohort of Breuci, sub-curator of the Flaminian Way and doles, sub-curator of public works, Julia Lucilla, of senatorial rank (set this up), to her well-deserving husband: he lived 48 years, 6 months, 25 days.'

recovery of the money is promised a tenth of its value as a reward. In the Roman world it was up to the wronged person to bring a thief to justice and prosecute him in the courts. Where the thief was not known, it was very likely thought that the placing of a curse upon him might help in the initial detective processes. A curse which had been committed to the waters of the hot springs at Bath refers to the kidnapping of Vilbia. The deity is invited to liquefy the

**100** Curse inscribed on a lead sheet, found in the reservoir below the King's Bath at Bath. It reads in transposed form:

*Qui mihi Vilbiam involavit sic liquat comodo aqua. Ella muta qui eam voravit si Velvinna Exsupereus Verianus Severinus Augustalis Comitianus Catusminianus Germanilla Iovina*

'May he who carried off Vilbia from me become as liquid as water. (May) she who obscenely devoured her (become) dumb, whether Velvinna, Exsupereus, Severinus, Augustalis, Comitianus, Catusminianus, Germanilla (or) Jovina.'

captor, and there follows a list of possible suspects: Velvinna, Exsupereus, Verianus, Severinus, Augustalis, Comitianus, Catusminianus, Germanilla and Jovina. It is an interesting list, since it contains both male and female names, suggesting perhaps that Vilbia was the name of a slave, or possibly even of an animal. If she was neither, then the statements might almost appear to be a commentary on contemporary sexual practices.

Another source of information about the people of the province is the large collection of graffiti which were scratched or punched on a very wide variety of objects, such as ceramic or metal vessels, personal trinkets, building stones or wall-plaster. Mostly this was done simply to denote ownership of the object, such as the samian bowl and silver spoon, found together in a rubbish pit at the villa at Eccles in Kent, on which the name Januaris had been scratched. Sometimes simple messages or allusions were made, such as the oft-quoted piece of Italian red-gloss pottery from Leicester linking the names of Lucius, a gladiator, with Verecunda, possibly an actress. The writing of graffiti on walls is by no means a modern practice, but has a strong tradition in almost every literate society. Nothing yet discovered in Britain can compete with the many examples found in such places as Pompeii or Ostia, yet they still provide an interesting social commentary on Roman Britain. Obscene words or phrases were scratched on walls of a derelict house in the centre of Leicester and painted, possibly as part of the decoration, on the wall of a villa at Alresford (Essex); if the latter was indeed part of the original design, we might well wonder what it had incorporated. How, also, might we interpret the information imparted by the same Leicester source, that Civilis is imprisoned, or was he, alternatively, simply hiding?

This and the preceding chapter have been principally concerned with the introduction of the *dramatis personae* of Roman Britain, in such a way that they illustrate as much as possible of the activities of their daily lives, their careers, beliefs and personalities. Since there are many gaps in this form of evidence for Britain, it means that the resulting synthesis is by no means completely comprehensive. In this respect it must be remembered that much of the evidence required to fill these gaps has to be derived either from archaeological sources, which in the absence of inscriptions are essentially anonymous, or from analogies in other provinces. Although the net has been stretched as widely as possible, people mentioned in the latter category are not strictly relevant to this account as they were never inhabitants of, or even visitors to, Britain. The British evidence, allied with allusions to temporary or permanent residents of the province from outside, must therefore stand on its own.

# The benefit for Rome — Chapter eight
## a conclusion

We have seen in the earlier chapters something of the people who lived and worked in Roman Britain, their way of life and the benefits and disadvantages which accrued to them from the Roman occupation. In conclusion, we may briefly review the cost to Rome of the maintenance of the British province and the profits obtained from it.

The cost of upkeep was considerable. As already indicated in Chapter 4, Britain, for its size, contained one of the largest garrisons of any province in the empire. A rough computation — it is not possible on the available evidence to be more accurate — shows that, at the time of Domitian, when Agricola was conducting his northern campaigns, the annual wages alone of the army almost certainly exceeded 13 million denarii. The figure is probably conservative, but still represents a very considerable sum of money. Add to it almost any figure one cares to think of to cover the remaining expenses of the governor and his staff, the procurator and his staff, occasional grants to, or remission of taxes from, municipalities, and the cost of raw materials and equipment, and it likely that a sum approaching 20 million denarii, equivalent to some 90,000 kg of silver, would have been needed annually to run the province. To the financial cost must be added the almost permanent drain on the empire's manpower resources. The frontiers of Britain were seldom at peace, resulting, if not always in a flood, then at least in a constant trickle of casualties needing replacement, to which must also be added the vacancies caused in the ranks by retirement. There is no doubt that this problem became much aggravated towards the end of the second century and remained in being until the end of the occupation.

So much for the debit side; by what did Rome profit, and did this profit balance the cost? In the first place there was probably a psychological gain simply caused by the capture of Britain; the morale of the conqueror is invariably improved by success. Strategically also the frontiers of Britain, expensive though they were to maintain, must be set against a wider background and not viewed purely in local terms. They acted as the frontiers of north-west Gaul and, to a lesser extent, Spain and so allowed peaceful and profitable life to develop in these provinces, as well as in lowland Britain, largely unhindered by military interference. Had this not been so, then the maintenance of a frontier along the Channel coast of Gaul would almost certainly have been more expensive both in terms of cash and manpower; moreover total revenue would have been correspondingly reduced. The invasion of Britain brought with it not only an increase in the supply of slaves, resulting directly from the warfare, but also, in the longer term, a boost to recruitment for the army in the occupied areas, so to some extent helping to neutralise the drain on manpower which was simultaneously taking place. The occupation also provided a large population who had to pay taxes, both in cash and in kind, so spreading the cost of upkeep of the north-western frontier garrisons over a far wider area. Moreover, the extra territory which was annexed helped to produce food and materials for those same garrisons and so again spread the burden of supply. We have no information on the amount of tax which the British people contributed, so we cannot tell if they could by themselves have carried the cost of the army and the administration stationed in the province.

Other benefits directly accruing to Rome were those derived from the exploitation of mineral resources and those from the various activities of the imperial estates, land owned by the emperor. Although Britain possessed deposits of all the commonly used metals, it seems unlikely that silver production could ever have reached the level of 90,000 kg annually required to pay for the armed forces and other expenditure under Domitian. Nevertheless the silver deposits were a not insignificant part of the empire's total resources and came into their own in the later fourth century, along with tin. Britain also provided a new and largely unexploited market for goods from elsewhere in the empire and so, through the widening activities of merchants, and the additional taxes which they consequently paid, helped to increase imperial revenues, further swollen in turn by customs duties exacted on the goods passing the frontiers or the provincial boundaries. In turn also, the empire profited further by the goods which were produced in Britain and then exported to other provinces or beyond the frontiers, although there was probably very little in Britain which could not have been equally well provided from elsewhere.

Can we, on this information, assess Britain as a profitable province? If all the factors are considered together then it probably was, making it worth the several tens of thousands of millions of denarii sunk in it over the period of occupation. Only once apparently did Roman resolve falter when, under Nero, there was talk of abandonment, but even then it was deemed to be a too-costly operation. For the remainder, proof of the value of Britain to Rome comes in the subsequent events. Thrice Britain seceded from the empire on account of the personal ambitions of officers or governors and thrice was recovered by the central authority in Rome. On at least three other occasions it was subjected to severe invasions from outside and suffered several internal rebellions, and each time considerable efforts were made to expel the invaders, or crush the rebels, and set matters right. Yet in some ways Britain was as isolated from the heart of the empire as the eastern provinces which were subjugated by Trajan and so soon afterwards abandoned by Hadrian. It was almost more isolated, and possibly less wealthy, than Dacia, yet that province was never recovered after the barbarian invasions of the later third century. Indeed, Britain remained a province until the break-up of the western empire in the early fifth century, and even then there survived a desire, fostered by Britons on one side and the Church in Rome on the other, so to remain, despite the military impossibility of achieving it. Few of the measures to guard British security over the years would have been taken had Rome developed any serious doubts on the wisdom of retaining the province as part of her empire. We should therefore conclude that Rome could not do without Britain and that, considered as a whole, there was greater profit than loss.

# The best of
# early Roman Britain

### Selected sites of the Iron Age and early Roman periods to visit in Britain

Places marked with an asterisk have a museum on the site.

### Urban

Ancaster, Lincs. (SK 9843)
South-east corner of defences visible as earthworks.
* Aldborough, Yorks. (SE 4066)
Sections of the defences and internal buildings exposed.
* Bath, Somerset (ST 7564)
Spa and associated baths.
Caerwent, Mon. (ST 4690)
Most of the circuit of the walls, with gates and external bastions still standing to a considerable height.
Caistor-by-Norwich, Norfolk (TG 2303)
Circuit of defences mostly visible as earthworks; internal features sometimes show as crop-marks.
Chesterton, Warwicks. (SP 3459)
Line of defences visible as earthworks.
* Cirencester, Glos. (SP 0201)
Section of the north-east wall exposed; amphitheatre visible as an earthwork.
* Colchester, Essex (TL 9925)
Circuit of walls; Balkerne (west) gate; north-east gate; also defences of Iron Age *oppidum*.
* Dorchester, Dorset (SY 6990)
Amphitheatre; internal buildings at Colliton Park exposed.
Great Casterton, Leics. (TF 0009)
North-east corner of defences visible as earthworks.
* Leicester, Leics. (SK 5804)
Jewry wall and parts of bath-house exposed.
* Lincoln, Lincs. (SK 9771)
Sections of defences of both upper and lower towns. Newport Arch (north gate); east and south-west gates exposed.
Silchester, Hants. (SU 6462)
Circuit of walls; internal features sometimes seen as crop-marks and earthworks; amphitheatre; also sections of defences of Iron Age *oppidum*.
* Verulamium, Herts. (TL 1307)
Circuit of walls; internal buildings; theatre; also sections of defences of Iron Age *oppidum*.
* Wall, Staffs. (SK 1006)
Parts of *mansio*, including bath-house, exposed.
Wroxeter, Salop. (SJ 5608)

Bath-house and associated buildings; part of forum; sections of
the defences visible as earthworks.
* York, Yorkshire (SE 6052)
See military sites.

## Iron Age hill-forts and *oppida* (see also Urban sites)
Bigbury, Kent (TR 117575)
Sections of defences, particularly on the north side, visible in
woodland.
Hod Hill, Dorset (ST 857106)
Hill-fort with Roman auxiliary fort in north-west corner; some
hut circles still visible.
Maiden Castle, Dorset (SY 669885)
Hill-fort of great size.
Stanwick, Yorks. (NZ 1811)
*Oppidum* with sections of defences still visible.

## Rural
Beadlam, Yorks. (SE 6384)
Villa with parts visible.
Bignor, Sussex (SU 9814)
Villa with parts visible.
* Chedworth, Glos. (SP 0513)
Villa with parts visible.
Ewe Close, Cumbria (NY 6013)
Native village visible as earthworks.
Brading, I.O.W. (SZ 5986)
Villa with parts visible.
* Fishbourne, W. Sussex (SU 8303)
Supposed palace of King Cogidubnus.
* Lullingstone, Kent (TA 5365)
Villa with parts visible.
Chisenbury Warren, Wilts. (SU 179538)
Native village visible as earthworks.

## Military
Ardoch, Tayside (NN 8410)
Auxiliary fort and campaign camps visible as earthworks.
Birrens, Dumfries and Galloway (NY 2175)
Auxiliary fort with gates still standing.
Borough-by-Bainbridge, North Yorks. (SD 9390)
Auxiliary fort visible as earthworks.
Burnswark, Dumfries and Galloway (NY 1878)
Practice siege camps flanking an Iron Age hill-fort.
Brecon-Gaer, Brecon (SO 0029)
Auxiliary fort with fortifications exposed.
* Caerleon, Mon. (ST 3390)
Legionary fortress, with some areas exposed; amphitheatre.
Blaen-Cwm-Bach, West Glam. (SS 7998)
Campaign camp.
* Chester, Cheshire (SJ 4066)
Legionary fortress. Circuit of the defences; amphitheatre;
Roodee Wall.
Chew Green, Northumberland (NY 8398)
Fortlet and series of campaign camps visible as earthworks.

Hardknott, Cumbria (NY 2101)
Auxiliary fort with visible parade ground outside.
High Rochester, Northumbria (NY 8398)
Auxiliary fort with some defences still standing.
Hod Hill, Dorset (ST 8510)
Vexillation fort in corner of Iron Age hill-fort.
Inchtuthill, Tayside (NO 1239)
Legionary fortress; outlines show as low embankments.
* Malton, Yorks. (SE 7971)
Auxiliary fort.
* Richborough, Kent (TR 3260)
Beach-head defences overlain by triumphal monument and
Saxon Shore fort.
Stainmore Pass, Yorks.-Cumbria (NY 7914 to NZ 0813)
Road with signal stations (Roper Castle, Bowes Moor and
Maiden Castle) and campaign camps visible as earthworks.
Whitley Castle, Northumberland (NY 6948)
Auxiliary fort.
* York, Yorks. (SE 6052)
Legionary fortress. Circuit of defences; headquarters building
(under Minster).

### Frontier works
Antonine Wall (NS 4673 to NT 0280)
Good sections visible at: Watling Lodge (NS 8679); Rough Castle
(NS 8479); latter also site of fort.
Hadrians Wall (NZ 223627 to NY 3066)
Good sections visible at: Birdoswald (NY 615664); Wall Town
Crags (NY 675665); Cawfields Milecastle (NY 715667); Turret 26B
at Brunton House (NY 922698).
Forts at:
Carrawburgh, Northumberland (NY 8751)
Fort visible as earthworks. Temple of Mithras laid out near south-
west corner.
* Chesterholm, Northumberland (NY 7766)
Parts of internal buildings exposed. Site of recent excavations in
the attached *vicus*.
* Chesters, Northumberland (NY 9170)
Many of the internal buildings are exposed; also extra-mural
bath-house. Abutment of bridge over North Tyne nearby (NY
915701).
* Corbridge, Northumberland (NY 9864)
Stanegate fort to rear of wall; later an important arsenal situated
within a large town. Many buildings exposed.
* Housesteads, Northumberland (NY 7868)
Fortifications, internal buildings in both fort and *vicus* exposed.
Nearby to the east lies the Knag Burn customs gateway (NY
7969).

### Communications, industrial centres and other remains
Dolocauthi, Carmarthen (SN 6640)
Site of Roman gold mines. Aqueducts serving the works and
settlement still visible on hillside above and to the north-east.
Dover, Kent (TR 3241)
Light-house situated on the cliff-top within the walls of the
medieval castle.

Helpringham, Lincs. (TF 1540)
Artificial drainage channel known as the Car Dyke visible at its
best here.
Lincoln – Good sections of Roman road can be seen both north
and south of the town running in north from SK 973797 to 972827,
in south from SK 985626 to 990496.
Bartlow Hills, Essex (TL 5844)
Tumuli of the early Roman period.
Charterhouse-in-Mendip, Avon (ST 5056)
Roman silver/lead mines; amphitheatre.

# Further reading

## Chapters 1—3

There are now a number of excellent and up-to-date sources for a more detailed account of the Iron Age in Britain and Western Europe. The opening chapters of S. S. Frere, *Britannia* (London, 1978 edn) provide a good introduction to the political, social and cultural history of the period, while B. W. Cunliffe, *Iron Age Communities in Britain* (London, 1974; revised edn 1978) and D. W. Harding, *The Iron Age in Lowland Britain* (London, 1974) provide a much more detailed treatment. Still of value on some specific problems are S. S. Frere (ed.), *Problems of the Iron Age in Southern Britain* (London, 1961) which contains a paper of key importance, by the late Derek Allen, on Iron Age coinage, and A. L. F. Rivet (ed.), *The Iron Age in Northern Britain* (Edinburgh, 1966).

Essential also for the geography of the period is the Ordnance Survey, *Map of Southern Britain in the Iron Age* (Chessington, 1967). Collections of essays on hill-forts by various authors are published in D. W. Harding (ed.), *Hillforts* (London, 1976) and Margaret Jesson and David Hill (eds), *The Iron Age and its Hillforts* (Southampton, 1971); the latter consists of papers read at a conference in honour of the late Sir Mortimer Wheeler, held at Southampton in 1971. Similarly, B. Cunliffe and T. Rowley (eds), *Oppida in Barbarian Europe* (Oxford, 1976) is a collection of papers presented at a conference in Oxford in 1975.

Of contemporary sources, Caesar's *De Bello Gallico* (available in a Penguin translation) is fundamental to the earliest of the periods considered in this book. Strabo in his *Geography* (available in translation in the Loeb Classical Library) adds a little to our knowledge, while Cassius Dio in his *History of Rome* (also in the Loeb Classical Library), written some 200 years after Caesar's expeditions, gives a brief account which was probably copied from the *Gallic Wars*, and adds some comments of his own.

## Chapter 4

The military conquest and subsequent occupation of Britain has been the subject of a huge quantity of recent literature. The present writer's *Roman Britain* (London, 1978) contains a slightly fuller version than presented here, and includes references to the organisation and works of the Roman army. But the fullest and most up-to-date account covering the whole period is contained in the relevant chapters of S. S. Frere, *Britannia* (London, 1978 edn) which may be supplemented by the more detailed treatment of differing viewpoints and specific topics in a number of books and articles. For the early conquest D. R. Dudley and G. Webster, *The Roman Conquest of Britain, AD 43–57* (London, 1965) and, by the second author, *Boudica* (London, 1978), together with two articles by Graham Webster may be recommended: 'The Claudian Frontiers of Britain' in *Studien zu den Militärgrenzen Roms* (proceedings of the VIth International Congress of Roman Frontier Studies, Cologne, 1967) and 'The Military Situation in Britain between AD 43 and 71' in *Britannia*, i (1970).

The later first and second centuries are covered between them by two articles by Brian Hartley: 'Roman York and the Northern Military Command to the Third Century AD' in R. M. Butler (ed.), *Soldier and Civilian in Roman Yorkshire* (Leicester, 1971) and 'The Roman Occupations of Scotland: The Evidence of the Samian Ware', in *Britannia*, iii (1972).

Alternative views of this vexed period of Romano-British history are put forward by M. G. Jarrett and J. C. Mann, 'Britain from Agricola to Gallienus' in *Bonner Jahrbuch*, 170 (1970) and by J. P. Gillam and J. C. Mann, 'The Northern British Frontier from Antoninus Pius to Caracalla' in *Archaelogia Aeliana*, xlviii (4th series 1970). Sources of evidence for the northern frontier are conveniently collected in J. C. Mann (ed.), *The Northern Frontier in Britain from Hadrian to Honorius: Literary and Epigraphical Sources* (Newcastle, undated). Imperial frontier policy in general is covered in an excellent article by J. C. Mann, 'The Frontiers of the Principate' in H. Temporini (ed.), *Aufstieg und Niedergang der Römischen Welt*, Vol. II, 1 (Berlin, 1974). More specifically, both frontiers of Hadrian's Wall and the Antonine Wall have maps of their respective areas published by the Ordnance Survey.

Among the remaining mass of literature may also be mentioned: D. R. Wilson, *Roman Frontiers of Britain* (London, 1967), a simple guide to the frontier works and their history; J. Collingwood Bruce, *Handbook to the Roman Wall* (13th edn, C. M. Daniels, Newcastle, 1978), an ideal guide-book to the sites on Hadrian's Wall taken in order from east to west; D. J. Breeze and B. Dobson, *Hadrian's Wall* (Harmondsworth, 1978), which despite its title, contains material applying to both frontiers, and to the Roman Army in general; A. S. Robertson, *The Antonine Wall* (Glasgow, 1968), which is modelled on the companion work for the Hadrianic frontier by Collingwood Bruce; an article 'John Horsley and the Antonine Wall' by K. Steer in *Archaeologia Aeliana*, xlii (4th series, 1964). Further papers relevant to the Antonine frontier and to the occupation of Scotland are to be found in *Scottish Archaeological Forum*, No. 7 (Edinburgh, 1975) and *Glasgow Archaeological Journal*, 4 (1976).

The Roman occupation of Wales is best summarised in V. E. Nash-Williams, *The Roman Frontier in Wales* (2nd edn, M. G. Jarrett, Cardiff, 1969), which includes both an historical and topographical account, fort by fort.

Among ancient writers, the best surviving account of the invasion of AD 43, although not strictly contemporary, is by Cassius Dio, *History of Rome* (Loeb Classical Library), while the Boudiccan rebellion and the events of that time and immediately thereafter are mentioned by Tacitus in his two works *The Life of Agricola* and *The Annals* (both available in Penguin translations and the Loeb Classical Library). R. M. Ogilvie and I. A. Richmond (ed.), *Cornelii Taciti de vita Agricolae* (Oxford, 1967), while not providing a translation, provides many additional and useful comments and attempts to relate the text to the archaeology. Cassius Dio also writes in brief on events of the second and early third centuries.

**Chapter 5**

Excellent short surveys of urban and rural aspects of Roman Britain are contained in S. S. Frere, 'Verulamium and the Towns of Britannia' and A. L. F. Rivet, 'The Rural Economy of Roman Britain', both included in H. Temporini and W. Haase (eds), *Aufstieg und Niedergang der Römischen Welt*, Vol. II, 3 (Berlin, 1975). Further consideration to both aspects is also given in S. S. Frere, *Britannia* (London, 1978 edn). For a fuller and more individual consideration of the major towns and for some of the problems associated with their understanding, see J. S. Wacher, *The Towns of Roman Britain* (London, 1978) and J. S. Wacher (ed.), *The Civitas Capitals of Roman Britain* (Leicester, 1975). The smaller settlement sites and minor towns are considered by M. Todd in an article 'The Small Towns of Roman Britain' in *Britannia*, i (1970) and in a collection of papers presented to an Oxford Conference in 1975: W. Rodwell and T. G. Rowley (eds), *The Small Towns of Roman Britain* (Oxford, 1976). Individual towns, or parts of them, have been dealt with by G. C. Boon, *Silchester, the Roman Town of Calleva* (Newton Abbot, 1974), B. Cunliffe, *Roman Bath* (Oxford, 1969), S. S. Frere, *Verulamium* I (Oxford, 1972), M. R. Hull, *Roman Colchester* (Oxford, 1958), R. Merrifield, *Roman London* (London, 1969): all rely heavily on, or are, excavation reports.

The countryside of Roman Britain is well summarised by S. Appelbaum in H. P. R. Finberg (ed.), *The Agrarian History of England and Wales* I, ii (Cambridge, 1972). In addition, villas form the central part of such publications as K. Branigan, *The Roman Villa in South-West England* (Bradford on Avon, 1977); A. L. F. Rivet (ed.), *The Roman Villa in Britain* (London, 1969); M. Todd (ed.), *Studies in the Romano-British Villa* (Leicester, 1978). An interesting and provocative study about a villa and its estate is provided by K. Branigan, *Gatcombe Roman Villa* (Oxford, 1977). The native aspect of rural life is better represented in A. C. Thomas (ed.), *Rural Settlement in Roman Britain* (London, 1966) and C. W. Phillips (ed.), *The Fenland in Roman Times* (London, 1970). The standard work on Roman roads in Britain remains I. D. Margary, *Roman Roads in Britain* (London, 1976), to which can now usefully be added the wider treatment accorded by R. Chevallier, *Roman Roads* (London, 1976). Industry has nowhere yet been thoroughly and systematically dealt with, but various facets of pottery production and distribution are contained in A. Detsicas (ed.), *Current Research in Romano-British Coarse Pottery* (London, 1973) and J. Dore and K. Greene (eds), *Roman Pottery Studies in Britain and Beyond* (Oxford, 1977). Of interest also in an industrial context is J. P. Wild, *Textile Manufacture in the Northern Roman Provinces* (Cambridge, 1970).

Religion and art are well considered, if not in great detail, in some of the general books (see also below) such as Frere's *Britannia*. To them can be added Stuart Piggott, *The Druids* (Harmondsworth, 1977); M. J. T. Lewis, *The Temples of Roman Britain* (Cambridge, 1966); E. and J. R. Harris, *The Oriental Cults of Roman Britain* (Leiden, 1965); Anne Ross, *Pagan Celtic Britain* (London, 1974); J. M. C. Toynbee, *Art in Roman Britain* (London, 1962) and, by the same author, *Art in Britain under the Romans* (Oxford, 1964). Burial customs in the Roman world are also discussed by J. M. C. Toynbee, *Death and Burial in the Roman World* (London 1971) and, more specifically to Britain, R. Reece (ed.), *Burial in the Roman World* (London, 1977).

## Chapters 6 and 7

Central to the theme adopted by these chapters is R. G. Collingwood and R. P. Wright, *The Roman Inscriptions of Britain*, vol. I (Oxford, 1965). Unfortunately, the volume on *instrumentum domesticum* has not yet appeared, and for these the reader must, therefore, turn to *Corpus Inscriptionum Latinarum*, vol. VII, for Britain, with the supplementary information contained in various volumes of *Ephemeris Epigraphica* and the annual summaries recording the discovery of new inscriptions in the *Journal of Roman Studies*, from 1910–69, thereafter in successive volumes of *Britannia*. Helpful also are A. R. Burn, *The Romans in Britain* (Oxford, 1969) and N. Lewis and M. Reinhold, *Roman Civilization, Sourcebook II: The Empire* (New York, 1966). Two publications by the London Association of Classical Teachers: *Some Inscriptions from Roman Britain* (London, 1969) and J. C. Mann and R. G. Penman (eds), *Literary Sources for Roman Britain* (London, 1977) are equally valuable. Many of the inscriptions quoted from continental sources but relating to Britain will be found in H. Dessau, *Inscriptiones Latinae Selectae* (Berolini, 3 vols, 1892–1916), or in other volumes of *Corpus Inscriptionum Latinarum*, notably volumes VI, XI–XIV. The governors of Britain are extensively treated by A. R. Birley, 'The Roman Governors of Britain' in *Epigraphische Studien,* 4 (1967). Also of interest with regard to the northern part of the province is P. Salway, *The Frontier People of Roman Britain* (Cambridge, 1965).

## General

In addition to the foregoing there are a number of books of a general nature. I. A. Richmond, *Roman Britain* (Harmondsworth, 1963); A. L. F. Rivet, *Town and Country in Roman Britain* (London, 1965) and A. R. Birley, *Life in Roman Britain* (London, 1972) are excellent introductions to the subject, while R. G. Collingwood (ed. I. A. Richmond), *The Archaeology of Roman Britain* (London, 1969) contains a more detailed treatment of different types of site. J. Liversidge, *Britain in the Roman Empire* (London, 1968) covers many of the social and economic aspects, making extensive use of analogies from other provinces. As a reference book containing entries of discoveries down to the mid-1950s, W. Bonser, *A Romano-British Bibliography* (Oxford, 1964) is invaluable, as is the Ordnance Survey's *Map of Roman Britain* now in a new edition (Chessington, 1979). Annual archaeological discoveries, as well as inscriptions, have been recorded briefly since 1970 in the journal *Britannia*, which also contains many useful articles on Iron Age, Roman and Dark Age Britain; before 1970 the summaries are to be found in successive volumes of the *Journal of Roman Studies*. From time to time, also, papers relating to Roman Britain are published in the *Antiquaries Journal, Archaeological Journal, Archaeologia, Antiquity* and in the transactions or journals of the various county societies. Abstracts of many of the more important papers can be found in the Council for British Archaeology, *British Archaeological Abstracts*, published twice yearly.

# Index

Page numbers in bold type refer to illustrations and their captions.

192